Sámi Education

Pigga Keskitalo / Kaarina Määttä / Satu Uusiautti

Sámi Education

Bibliographic Information published by the Deutsche Nationalbibliothek
The Deutsche Nationalbibliothek lists this publication in the Deutsche Nationalbibliografie; detailed bibliographic data is available in the internet at http://dnb.d-nb.de.

Printed with financial support of the University of Lapland

Cover Design:
© Olaf Gloeckler, Atelier Platen, Friedberg

Library of Congress Cataloging-in-Publication Data

Keskitalo, Pigga, 1972-
  Sámi education / Pigga Keskitalo, Kaarina Määttä, Satu Uusiautti.
    pages cm.
  Includes bibliographical references.
  ISBN 978-3-631-62597-2
  1. Sami (European people)—Education. 2. Sami (European people)—Social conditions. 3. Sami (European people)—Research. 4. Education, Bilingual—Europe, Northern—Research. 5. Sami language—Study and teaching. I. Title.
  DL42.L36K47 2013
  371.829'9457—dc23
                                                    2013014986

ISBN 978-3-631-62597-2
© Peter Lang GmbH
Internationaler Verlag der Wissenschaften
Frankfurt am Main 2013
All rights reserved.
Peter Lang Edition is an Imprint of Peter Lang GmbH.

Peter Lang – Frankfurt am Main · Bern · Bruxelles · New York · Oxford · Warszawa · Wien

All parts of this publication are protected by copyright. Any utilisation outside the strict limits of the copyright law, without the permission of the publisher, is forbidden and liable to prosecution. This applies in particular to reproductions, translations, microfilming, and storage and processing in electronic retrieval systems.

www.peterlang.de

Forewords

The special needs of indigenous peoples' education have aroused interest ever since the educational sovereignty has started to come true across the world. Therefore, it is more topical than ever to develop indigenous pedagogies. We too want to seize the challenge: the task of this book is to contribute to the educational challenges among indigenous peoples by introducing research results, educational special features, and future trends.

Sámi Education is aimed at everyone who is interested in educational conditions among indigenous peoples. The especial target group is students of education; teachers and educators at various school levels; educational, schooling, social, and health care administrative authorities; and Sámi children's parents—all people who have to deal with indigenous issues, pluralism, and multilingualism in diverse contexts. In addition, we hope that research institutions and universities and researchers who study indigenous peoples and cultures from various points of view would find the information provided by this book useful. The idea of the book originates in our joint discussions aiming ambitiously at producing information about the multi-faceted educational processes serving many needs and contexts of indigenous and western societies.

This book is divided into five chapters which include special viewpoints to Sámi research and education. The first chapter provides a glance at the history of Sámi education and the Sámi as an indigenous people. All historical happenings are intertwined in the assimilation processes during which some of the Sámi people have lost their cultural and linguistic special features. The second chapter concentrates on Sámi school research. We will introduce possibilities of doing ethnographic research in indigenous school contexts. Indigenous school research also involves certain ethical elements that must be recognized. The third chapter introduces the special features of Sámi education. We will provide research-based information about the practical framework of Sámi education and discuss the linguistic and cultural characteristics that should be given special attention in education. The fourth chapter brings out challenges and possibilities of Sámi language teaching. As the Sámi languages are endangered, Sámi language teaching and Sámi-speaking education require special pedagogical cultural-sensitive solutions that need to be noticed when planning, realizing, and evaluating education. The fifth chapter is oriented toward the future. Hence, we will discuss how to secure the Sámi language and what would be the key solutions of Sámi education. The aim is to introduce models that are to provide viewpoints and foundation for finding educational solutions for the sustainable future.

The book is based on our peer-refereed scientific articles that have been published in international journals. The articles that function as the basis of the book were molded so that they form a harmonious entity. In all, the ultimate purpose of the book is to become aware of the practices of indigenous education through scientific research. The book is written by Associate Professor, Dr. Pigga Keskitalo (Ph.D.) from the Sámi University College, Norway; and Professor, Dr. Kaarina Määttä (Ph.D.) and Specialist, Dr. Satu Uusiautti (Ph.D.) from the University of Lapland, Finland.

We want to express our warm thanks to the teachers and students for giving the opportunity of shedding light on the special features of Sámi education. We thank Secretary Heli Niskala for her help with the formatting of the book. Furthermore, we want to thank our academic work places, Sámi University College and University of Lapland, for supporting our research. Giitu olu buohkaide doarjagis!

In Enontekiö and Rovaniemi, on the Sámi's national day, 6 Feb 2013

Pigga Keskitalo   Kaarina Määttä   Satu Uusiautti

Table of Contents

Forewords	5
Publication Details of the Articles	8
A Glance at the Roots of Sámi Education	9

Sámi Research

1. The Prospects of Ethnography at the Sámi School	13
2. Ethical Perspectives on Sámi School Research	29

Special Traits of Sámi Education

3. How do the Sámi Culture and School Culture Converge – or do they?	39
4. Toward the Practical Framework of Sámi Education	47

Sámi Language Teaching

5. A View on Sámi Language Teaching	59
6. The Linguistic Special Features of the Sámi Education	71
7. "Language Immersion Tepee" as a Facilitator of the Sámi Language Learning	79

An Eye to the Future of Sámi Education

8. Making the Dream of a Sámi School Come True: Voices from the Field	83
9. Sámi Pedagogy	95
References	99
Authors	119

Publication Details of the Articles

Keskitalo, P., Määttä, K., & Uusiautti, S.. (2011). The prospects of ethnography at the Sámi School. *Journal of Studies in Education, 1*, 1–30.

Keskitalo, P., Määttä, K., & Uusiautti, S. (2012). Ethical perspectives on Sámi School Research. *International Journal of Education, 4*(4), 267-283. doi: 10.5296/ije.v4i4.2908

Keskitalo, P., & Määttä, K. (2011). How do the Sámi culture and school culture converge - or do they? *The Australian Journal of Indigenous Education, 40*, 112-119. doi: 10.1375/ajie.40.112

Keskitalo, P., Määttä, K., & Uusiautti, S. (2011). Toward practical framework of Sámi education. *British Journal of Educational Research, 1*, 84-106. doi: 10.5296/jse.v1i1.911

Keskitalo, P., & Määttä, K. (2011). The linguistic special features of the Sámi education. *Indian Journal of Applied Linguistics, 37*, 5-26.

Keskitalo, P., Uusiautti, S., & Määttä, K. (2012). In the name of cultural sensitivity – A view on Sámi language teaching. *Academic Journal of Social Sciences, 1*(1), 1-9.

Määttä, K., Keskitalo, P., & Uusiautti, S. (2013). Making the dream of a Sámi School come true: voices from the field. *Journal of Language Teaching and Research, 3*.

A Glance at the Roots of Sámi Education

The Sámi as Indigenous People

Sápmi means the geographical area populated traditionally by the Sámi people. The Sámi live in four countries: in Northern Finland, Sweden, Norway, and Kola Peninsula in Russia. Altogether, there are about 100,000 Sámi people in these countries. About 40,000 of them can speak the Sámi languages. The Sámi people form a nationality that does not have a nation or nation borders but a common based language, culture, and history (Smith, 2006). The Sámi language belongs to Finno-Ugrian languages. Nine Sámi languages are left in Nordic countries and Russia, and all of them are endangered (Magga & Skutnabb-Kangas, 2001) partly as there has been going on an assimilation process for centuries.

The Sámi are descendants of the people who first inhabited the northern Fennoscandinavia shortly after the end of the last ice age, approximately 10 000 years ago. Historically, the Sámi have been divided by livelihood and region into reindeer herders, fishermen, and forest Sámi (Halinen, 2011). The Sámi society was to face increasingly drastic changes caused by outsiders from the 16th century onward. The Nordic countries started to take control of the land of the Sámi by religious conversion, supporting settlement and replacing the Sámi administration with an external administrative system. Due to the western settlement in the Nordic countries, the Sámi became a minority in most of their traditional areas (Josefsen, 2010).

Sápmelaččat, in other words the Sámi, are an indigenous people. The concept of "indigenous people" is defined for example in the ILO convention number 169. According to the convention, indigenous people are descended from the population that inhabited the area at the time when the country was colonized or when the modern state was established. In addition, the population must identify itself as an indigenous people (ILO, 1989). However, definitions are interpretive. The Sámi have preserved their linguistic, cultural, and communal special features at least partly separate from the surrounding dominant culture. According to the ILO convention, these features are also one criterion for being an indigenous people. Of the countries with a Sámi population, Norway is the only one that has ratified ILO's agreement on indigenous peoples.

In Norway, the Sámi's right to preserve their own language and develop it in various connections is written into the constitution (Grunnloven, § 110 a). Likewise, the Constitution of Finland guarantees the Sámi the right to maintain and develop their language and culture (The Constitution of Finland, 731/1999). The Parliament of Sweden recognized the Sámi as a people starting from 2010. The Constitution of Sweden states that the Sámi and ethnic, linguistic, and religious minorities have the right to maintain and develop their own cultural and societal life (Lag 2009:724). The Constitution of the Russian Federation (1993) includes a decree that concerns the protection of indigenous peoples. A number of major international instruments concern the Sámi people, such as the UN Declaration on Indigenous Peoples (2007).

The Sámi culture is not a coherent entity, but covers multiple societies and languages. Though, the Sámi maintain a unified culture by a national flag and celebrating Sámi People's Day. The Sámi parliaments in Norway, Sweden and Finland, serve as the authoritative advisory agency in issues regarding the Sámi people, but have no legal or executive power. The purpose of the Sámi Parliaments in Nordic countries inhabited by the Sámi people is to take care of the Sámi language, culture and issues regarding the Sámi's position as an indigenous people.

The History of Sámi Education

Christianity was introduced to the Sámi early, first in the 12th century and more powerfully again in the 17th century. The Christian church played a major role in western oppression and assimilation pressures targeted at the Sámi. The confrontation between the western and Sámi cultures was problematic (Kylli, 2005). In each country where the Sámi resided, the Sámi populations were subjected— through education and other means—to pressures of assimilation. The Sámi were pushed to give up their native language and start using the dominant language, change their values and lifestyle.

Five stages can be distinguished in the history of Sámi education: the mission period from 1600 to the end of the 19th century, the long period of assimilation into western culture from the 19th century to the end of the 1960s, the emphasis on bilingualism from the end of the 1980s, and the improvement of the position of the Sámi language after it became an official language the Sámi districts (Girko-, oahpahus- ja dutkandepartemeanta, 1995). The Second World War had ruinous effects to the Sámi education and language. The War's legacy left the Sámi without education in any language for several years, which negatively affected literacy rates and ability to transfer Sámi language to next generations (Anaya, 2011).

The ethnic and national awakening of the Sámi started in the late 19th century leading to the establishment of the first local Sámi associations and newspapers. An actual renaissance of the Sámi culture took place in the late 1960s as a result of a national awakening after long assimilation. However, it was not until 1997 when first steps toward autonomous Sámi education were taken by introducing the Sámi curriculum in Norway. Sweden had a Sámi curriculum in 2011.

Finland does not have a Sámi curriculum. At the moment, the structure and contents of Sámi education are finding their place and form.

The Research Data and Methods

In the studies on which this book is based, Sámi education was researched through ethnography and teachers' experiences of teachers aiming at eliciting structures related to power and otherness and that are also connected to the position and historical process of Sámi education. The purpose of educational research is to empower the indigenous community and bring out the voices of experts of Sámi education, teachers, and pupils. This book is based partly on Dr. Pigga Keskitalo's (2010) doctoral study *Cultural Sensitivity in The Sámi School through Educational Anthropology* about Sámi education in Norway. Her research data comprise observations and research diary on education provided in the Sámi- and Norwegian-speaking classes in six Sámi schools in Norway between 2001 and 2007, interviews of teachers and pupils, entries in the research journal, and school documents such as annual plans and curricula. The data were further analyzed given that ethnographic data are not thoroughly studied all at once, but can be reread in new contexts and through new perspectives (see Salo, 1999, pp. 11, 13). The situation of Sámi education was examined through two reforms: *Curriculum 1997 Sámi* (Gonagaslaš girko-, oahpahus- ja dutkandepartemeanta, 1997) and *Curriculum 2007 Sámi* (Máhttodepartemeanta et al., 2007). The Norwegian data were complemented by school ethnography (observations and interviews) performed in elementary instruction at five schools that provide Sámi language teaching in Finland (six Sámi teachers) between 2005 and 2008.

The third set of data was obtained at the first national Sámi Pedagogy Conference in Inari, Finland, in 2011 among people who work with Sámi education. The participants of the research (N= 64) participated in the conference and were asked to share their experiences of Sámi education. The participants were teachers from the schools and day care centers of the Sámi domicile area, local school authorities and representatives of the Finnish and Norwegian Sámi Parliaments and higher education. Our findings are based on a combination of methods that complement each other. Altogether, the data were not only abundant but also comprehensive and diversified. This book will have excerpts from various data to show the voices from the school field.

Research involving indigenous people is being undertaken by researchers, who bring forward worldviews that shape the approach of the research, the theoretical and conceptual frameworks, and the epistemology, methodology, and ethics. Many times such research bridges western practices and indigenous knowledge; however, bringing together these two worldviews can also present challenges. It might be challenging to find a way of bringing together Indigenous ways of knowing and western ways of conducting research, specifically qualitative inquiry (Lavallée, 2009). We try to meet this challenge as a research team that consists of both indigenous and non-indigenous researchers. Yet, we want to share our experiences and expertise to develop the field through our collaboration. We as researchers are aware of our position and want to show humble respect for this task as there is a wide range of challenges. Simultaneously, we know that there are educational developmental projects going on in each country with a Sámi population. We want to contribute to this discussion and to the growing scholarly work of bridging indigenous ways of knowing and western principles. As the continuation of the process, the findings are written back to the indigenous peoples and others interested in order to be able to influence and construct multiple educational contexts in collaboration.

The Prospects of Ethnography at the Sámi School

Educational research has become more and more versatile and traveled a long road from quantitative research toward various qualitative methods (Creswell, 2003; Henson et al., 2010). Ethnography has been recognized as a suitable method when the aim is to understand people and their life in the context they live (Hostetler, 2005). Given this starting point, ethnography is well applicable when doing research on indigenous peoples' cultures, education, and life. Institutions like school have come to serve as mediators between indigenous communities and the outside world, and they are sites in which scholars can contribute to community-based research without intruding on private life. Simultaneously, such institutions are ideal for the study of processes of, for example, self-representation, self-determination, and repatriation (Turner Strong, 2005).

Ethnography as a word is derived from a Greek word *"ethnos"* which refers to a tribe or people and a word *"graphia"* which means "to write" (Opas, 2004). Thus, ethnography aims to describe the nature of those who are studied (i.e. to describe a people, an ethnos) through writing. The roots of ethnography are in anthropology (Metsämuuronen, 2006)—and often among quite exotic and remote research targets. Polish Bronislaw Malinowski (1984) conducted research among the habitants of the island of Trobriant between 1913 and 1916 and made the concept of "field" in ethnographic research well-known. Ethnography can be defined in many ways. According to Clifford Geertz (1973), ethnography is thick description about culture (see also James, 2001); whereas Beverley Skeggs (1999a) defines it as a way of seeing otherwise. Paul Atkinson and Martin Hammersley (1994) compare it with an expedition during which the researcher works with unstructured material and is interested in the research target. Ethnographic research is a living process where the researcher has to accept threads that lead to several directions (Saikkonen & Miettinen, 2005).

Recently, more attention has been paid on how the western education has affected individuals, local culture, and knowledge. Along research, the forms of indigenous knowledge are beginning to be understood by scholars (Murillo, 2009)—even to the extent where methods of collecting, analyzing and presenting data characterize the western academic tradition as well as indigenous ways of knowing, communicating and sharing knowledge (Webster & John, 2010). In ethnography, interest has been focused on, for example, institutionalized education, learning of rituals, and the study of cultural and social structures (e.g., Ford, 1997; Pollock, 1997; Sindell, 1997; Spindler & Spindler, 1997a, 1997b). Indeed, when the purpose is to rethink schooling from the perspective of indigenous peoples' own needs, it is worth asking how educational practices and curriculum will need to change to recognize and incorporate local forms of knowledge and ways of knowing.

The new school of thought disassociates itself from the anthropologic tradition when it comes to research on education and schooling (see also Geertz, 1973, 2010; Smith, 2005) and aims at highlighting issues related to power relationships and epistemology. Our research aims at theoretizing and noticing the culture through its own premises. In this chapter, we will present analysis how to use ethnography in the indigenous context of Sámi education. Further, we review the typical features of ethnographic research and its applicability to the studying of Sámi education, and how the ethnographer's role in school ethnography is carried out at the indigenous people's schools and especially by a member of the indigenous people. Also the purpose of this chapter is to view what are the possibilities to elicit the Sámi school operation through ethnography by asking what kind of picture can be drawn of the Sámi School through ethnographic research.

School Ethnography among Indigenous Peoples

School ethnography has been implemented already for over three decades (Gordon et al., 2001). Everyone has some kinds of school experiences. Often, familiarity is considered problematic to the reliability of the research (Coffey, 1999). An ethnographer who conducts research at school has to be able to re-consider what is already known and safe (Gordon et al., 2001). Culturally appropriate research techniques should be utilized by the ethnographer, and in this regard, cultural sensitivity and competence are important (Castro, 2007).

It has described the Sámi culture from the outsider's point of view from the end of the 17th century till the end of the 20th century—this period was colored by colonialism, imperialism, nationalism, social Darwinism, and cultural racism (Schanche, 2002). When it comes to the Sámi, previously anthropologists wandered in Lapland researching initiated by outsiders (the most active lappologists were, for example, K. Nickul, T. I. Itkonen, J. K. Qvigstad, and K. B. Wiklund). It is worthwhile to notice the lappological tradition as a factor that affects Sámi research. Lappology is the antecedent of Sámi research and research on the Sámi people. However, the lappological research was conducted by outsiders in order to build the identities of the Norwegians, Finns, and Swedes simultaneously creating a picture of the Sámi as the opposite and other without any possibilities to survive in the modern world. Veli-Pekka Lehtola deliberated the connection between Sámi research and lappology in the following manner: All modern researchers are followers of the lappological tradition. The lappologists' role at their own time was not that black and white as is claimed. By deciphering the lappologists' real role in their own community, it is possible to study the present roles: the relationships between the researcher, scientific community, and society (cited in Vilkuna, 2005, p. 258). During the past decades, Sámi research has moved toward intercultural approach: the intent has been to replace the term "lappology" with a new appellation "multidisciplinary Sámi research" that also the Sámi participate in (Carpelan et al., 2004).

Sámi research is expected to be committed to benefit Sámi communities and on the other hand give an objective picture about Sámi culture. Before, the lappological tradition affected Sámi research. However, the lappological research was conducted by outsiders of the Sámi community in order to build their cultural identities simultaneously creating a picture of the Sámi as the opposite and other without any possibilities to survive in the modern world. During the past decades, Sámi research has moved toward an intercultural approach: the intent has been to replace the term lappology with a new appellation multidisciplinary Sámi research representing research in which the Sámi are proactive (Carpelan et al., 2004).

The macro-level problems of Sámi research relate to the colonization of the Sámi and affect directly to the micro-level. The features that are typical of school research effect in the background. One of the challenges in ethnography is to get access to the field as western researchers through history have met serious problems when trying to collect data in cultures different from their own. It condenses the core of ethnography that grounds on anthropology as this kind of approach can be seen problematic from indigenous peoples' point of view. For example, the school personnel do not necessarily trust that the research would improve the everyday situation at school. It can be called research skepticism which also bears the burden of lappology. Herewith, it can be difficult to find research participants. Yet, it is worth remembering that a teaching situation is—or at least should be—open by nature and that openness is the key word when aiming at developing school (Kohonen & Leppilampi, 1992). Indigenous people are generally cynical about the benefits of research and cautious toward what many perceive to be the colonial mentality or "positional superiority" ingrained in the psyche of western researchers (Prior, 2007).

Yet, the hallmark of traditional ethnographic research has been intensive, long-term participant-observation in a local community (Turner Strong, 2005), it is not the case in school research as the fieldwork is expected to last for reasonable period related to research ensemble. Despite increasing interest, school ethnography has it challenges as well. Ángel Díaz de Rada (2007) blames the school for being too bureaucratic in many ways in order to support ethnographic research as it is opposed to the positivist ideal of 'scientific' simplification (see also Erickson & Gutierrez, 2002). Whereas Martin G. Forsey (2010) points out how a reported sight is commonly considered objective in the western culture and suggest that researchers should apply engaged listening in addition to visual observation. In general, the idea about listening and giving space to indigenous peoples' opinions and experiences of education is essential. For example, Michael Marker (2000) claims that "if the stories of [indigenous] students could be heard and understood, and if the local political context of their encounter with higher education could be shown, it would unmask a number of presuppositions about ethnicity and education" (p. 401).

According to our literature survey, recent ethnographic research at indigenous peoples' schools seem to focus on decolonization and its manifestation at school through a variety of perspectives: for example, to identify both curriculum content and pedagogical strategy (London, 2002), culture-based curriculum (Hermes, 2000), the practical establishment of a school for indigenous people (Wardell, 2006), bilingual intercultural education in indigenous schools as an illustration of teacher interpretations of government policy (Valdiviezo, 2009), the dualistic notion of insider/outsider in ethnographic research (Webster & John, 2010), and physical education at indigenous peoples' school (Fitzpatrick, 2011). Research aims to implement the Sámi's self-determination because research can be seen as a way of enhancing self-direction, communal empowering, and finding functional strategies.

Natives or members of indigenous people have the advantage as they already have the same level with the research target that is other indigenous people; Ray Barnhardt (2002, p. 241) has quite incisively pointed out the difference between "ivory tower knowledge" and traditional, indigenous or real-world knowledge. Ole F. Lillemyr et al. (2010) have noted that for Indigenous people in particular, cultural values, sense of relatedness and self-determination are important components of school motivation. The ethnographic research approach can be used for analyzing and criticizing educational policy and its influence on the everyday life at school. The education policy and its impact on school everyday life can be analyzed and criticized by ethnographic research. Ethnographers can take advantage of their vantage point and participate in discussing contexts of their field (Gordon & Lahelma, 2004).

The Ethnographer at the Sámi School

The aim of the original empirical research was to analyze how the school culture and the Sámi culture converge (see Keskitalo, 2010). At the same time, the question of how the school supports the Sámi culture was at the center. The aim of the research is to emphasize the indigenous people's own meanings and dissect the culture from inside and from the point of view of the speakers of the Sámi language and bearers of the Sámi culture.

Based on practical experience and theoretical deliberation on ethnographic research at the Sámi School, the ethnographer's roles can be illustrated by introducing the roles of the ethnographer, and reviewing school ethnography among the Sámi through these roles (see *Figure 1*).

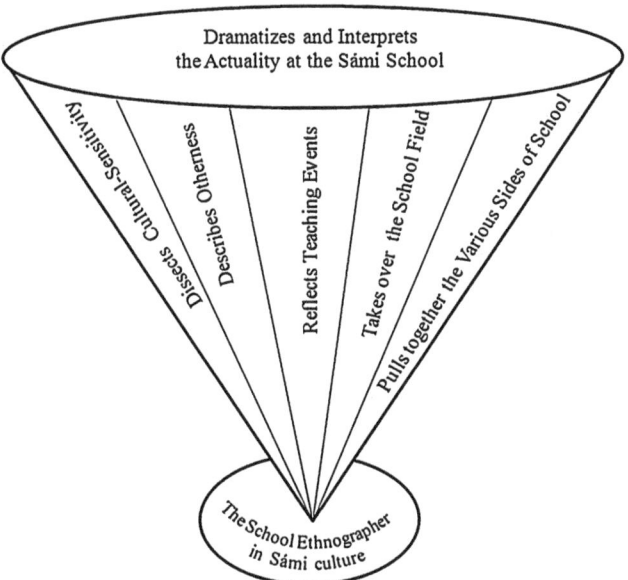

Fig. 1. The school ethnographer's roles in Sámi culture

The school ethnographer dissects cultural sensitivity

The main attention in Keskitalo's (2010) research was focused on the relation between socialization and enculturation because dovetailing the traditional and informal education and the role of the native culture is a central problem in education. The data showed that the way the school organizes the learning is not sufficient cultural sensitive as the western school culture dominates instruction in the Sámi School. Findings are spirally connected with the assimilation, power relations, and socialization processes that the Sámi experience and have gone through. The way the school organizes teaching is connected with the historical task of the school, the nature of the school as an organization, and the context in which Sámi schools provide their instruction. The challenge in many Sámi schools is that their pedagogical arrangements and curricula are similar to other schools. Students are not socialized into their own cultures in the wished amount.

The research material showed that the school culture and Sámi culture did not meet each other sufficiently. This phenomenon appears as liminalization where the Sámi School is on the way toward autonomy if the conditions are framed so that they will enable it. However, the question is not that simple: Rauna Kuokkanen (2007) writes about cultural conflicts by criticizing them. According to the author, we simply cannot talk about the collision of cultures because the issue is always linked with power relations as well.

The school ethnographer describes otherness

Ethnography and anthropological research tradition have been criticized especially for their focus on otherness and pursue of defining primitiveness. The research subjects were described as others, exciting and different. The other was seen as the opposite of oneself and the anthropologist's task was to explain the unfamiliarity into something understandable. The concept of otherness can be changed along with the change in ethnography. In the research on Sámi education, "the other" lives in the ethnographer's experiences and is researchable, interpretable, and understandable. Minna Opas (2004) considers ethnography as mutual understanding resulting from the negotiations between the ethnographer and research partners. The days at school consisted of numerous negotiation situations that included mutual experiences.

According to René Gothóni (1997), field work that involves data collection amid other people demands the ability to empathize and diverge. Empathizing means that the researcher tries to put herself in the research partners' position in order to understand them, their behavior, and the context where the Sámi schools operate. Yet, critical research also necessitates the ability to pull away from the research target. The aim is to view issues from further – this is why the ethnographer is supposed to keep a diary, write down observations, and read relevant literature.

Learning, knowing, and teaching are connected to the concept of otherness – through the roundabout way of unconscious social and cultural denial. Otherness does not speak frankly but it is substituted, displaces, or creates dreams that learning cannot handle directly. Unconscious otherness holds an indirect position in the interaction between a teacher and a pupil. It speaks by parentheses, replacement, denial, forgetting, rejection, fear, shame, and amusement. Otherness mirrors the repressive society and culture and it manifests itself in teacher-pupil interaction so that individuals repeat the macro-level practices in an institutional education situation (Ellsworth, 1997; see also Said, 1978).

The school ethnographer reflects teaching events

The research process is cyclic in nature. Its every phase involves analysis that proceeds as a reflective process all the way from planning till conclusions. The process in Keskitalo's (2010) research started with contextualization and formulating research questions that were specified into their final form during the research process. In order to contextualize the work, it was necessary to get acquaint with the history of Sámi education, its curricula and previous research on the curricula. In most educational research, reflection is defined as a useful and necessary method helping analyzing teaching and school environment critically. One way of doing this is through using observation and reflection as a way of bringing about change. In school research, reflection forms one important part of pursuing the change. In addition, reflection helps a researcher to demonstrate his/her own action and maturing, and his/her values and to reflect them in relation to the change (e.g. Oser et al., 1992; Artzt & Armour-Thomas, 2002).

The researcher reflects events that take place at school in order to perceive the present state of education. Therefore, reflection is a dialogue between questions and answers that researchers pose to themselves (e.g. Osterman & Kotkamp, 1993). It is also important to work in active co-operation with research partners and negotiate about research findings and estimate together whether the research findings describe the everyday situation and the experiences at schools. This was tested in Keskitalo's (2010) research many ways. She discussed continuously with teachers, parents, principals, pupils, other researchers and politicians and other interested about Sámi school situation so she could find out very wide picture about Sámi school's issues. She also sended her unfinished scripts to research partners to test her analysis. She also sended scientific articles she wrote for to get feedback for her final doctoral thesis. Research partners could also read interview transcribes. The research process was open and two-way so that everybody could learn during the process by reflecting teaching and learning at school.

The school ethnographer takes over the school field

When starting the field work, in the first phase, the field and its events observed are described by the ethnographer. In the next phase, the field is formed into writing that is not limited within the field and home any longer but is mixed with the various phases of the research and writing process (Atkinson, 1992; Gupta & Ferguson, 1996). In school ethnography, the time the researcher spends at school is not necessarily long but versatile data can form a triangulation in the research. Data triangulation refers to a multiple perspective in which various methods and approaches are combined (Saaranen-Kauppinen & Puusniekka, 2006). According to Ulla-Maija Salo (1999), the focus, analysis methods and the manner of representation have to specified and defined several times during ethnographic writing.

In Keskitalo's (2010) research, the relationship with knowledge was determined by social constructionist and the theory of post-structuralistic reading. Social constructionism means that knowledge is produced in cooperation with the research partners in a circular argument within the theory and that context where the Sámi School is located in. Furthermore, the post-structuralistic theory of reading was employed as it has emphasis on the event. Therefore, the ethics of reading refers to the sense of responsibility to the event and uniqueness. It means that firstly, the researcher has to be aware of her position. Secondly, the researcher cannot manifest what she has seen and experienced but merely, based on the research problems, bring out some practical challenges of the Sámi School. An ethnographer who researches the Sámi School has a structurally wide field to study: it includes students, teachers, text books, teaching arrangements, and the community outside the school. The ethnographer focuses on the everyday life at school in order to understand the daily practices and processes; and follows the events and teaching in the classroom by observation. Yet, it is impossible to observe everything that takes place in the field. Therefore, it is important that the researcher defines the limits for the analysis carefully.

Due to our findings the Sámi school research themes could be collected on the following themes (cf. Rantala, 2005):

(1) The school as material and economic environment (the equipment at school, learning materials),

(2) The school as physical space (school buildings, teachers' room, classrooms, break/playtime or PE facilities),

(3) The school as cultural and social environment (the cultural-sensitivity of school, the position of the school in the community),

(4) The school as linguistic and semantic environment (what language is used, how people talk about the school),

(5) The school as the environment for the interaction between people who work there (the interaction between teachers and students and other personnel, communication between the school and parents),

(6) The school as the learning environment constructed by teaching arrangements and learning situations (the number of students per classroom, timetables, the length of lessons, teaching methods, project and theme work),

(7) The school as space of discipline and control (the school regulations, means of controlling students).

The school ethnographer pulls together the various sides of school

One of the features in Keskitalo's (2010) research was the abundance of the phenomena in the indigenous peoples' teaching context: the connection between the teacher, teaching, guiding, and learning is complicated. Yet, the aim of classroom research is to perceive the connection of guiding and teaching with students' learning (Anderson & Burns, 1989) although it is challenging to describe all factors that affect the interaction between the teacher and the student group (Heikkilä & Sahlström, 2003; Sahlström, 2008a, 2008b). In addition, students' learning is a sum of several factors and it is not possible to completely or comprehensively observe the teacher's action in teaching (Anderson & Burns, 1989). Furthermore, ethnography can be suitable method for observing the unconscious work at classroom.

The purpose of ethnography is to create as comprehensive picture about the Sámi School and education as possible through diverse data collection: as if the ethnographer was assembling a jigsaw puzzle when conducting school research (see also Denzin & Lincoln, 2000). According to Neil Harrison (2005) indigenous students are already learning outside an assimilation of the position of a non-indigenous, usually western, teacher. This learning is produced through the discourse of negotiation, a meta-language that is produced outside the methodologies and theories and beyond the conscious mind of the student (see also Regalsky & Laurie, 2007).

The manifold nature of the context and many different approaches expose the research to disorder but it has to be considered as one characteristic of ethnography. Furthermore, the form and outline of the research are ambulatory concepts. In this process, the original research was molded into the present form. When dissecting the themes all over again, the approaches are different. According to Amanda Coffey (1999), the ethnographer's role has to be seen active, information productive and participative because of the social perspective of the field work.

In ethnographic school research, speech, actions, gestures, and movements are significant. As several conversations may take place in the classroom at the same time, the researcher has to select such entity that she finds out important enough to be documented. In the classroom, teaching happens formally through teaching arrangements and realization. In addition, various encounters and situations take place in the classroom and do not necessarily have anything to do with the formal teaching and learning. To the ethnographer, the context is a real challenge exactly because of the multidimensional activities in the classroom. It is also possible that acts and action are in danger of remaining ignored because people's speech and opinions come more clearly in the center. Indigenous peoples' schooling contexts are also multiple due to multicultural and –lingual contexts and this makes the school field within the demanding factors even more complicated to examine.

The school ethnographer dramatizes and interprets the actuality at the Sámi School

In ethnographic research, pictures, texts, conversations, and experiences are mixed up and form a new entity: an interpretation about what really happens at the Sámi School. Norman K. Denzin and Yvonna S. Lincoln (2000) use the term 'montage' to describe a stage where researchers place the pieces they use for describing the phenomenon they have studied. They situate actors on the research stage and select the actors' lines from the data. The drama is not authentic because researchers have selected the lines and scenes that represent the research target the best in their opinion. The happenings do not move on as a sequential continuum on stage but as various scenes and entrances into different situations. One of the most important tasks of the researchers and dramatizers is therefore editing (see Rantala, 2007).

The interpretation in Keskitalo's (2010) research revealed that the Sámi School did not appear very cultural sensitive. The problem of the school is that it cannot solve the ways how teaching is arranged in the western school world referring, for example, to teacher-centered teaching which is tied to text books. Subject and time allocation epitomizes this kind of the teaching arrangement as well. Organizing teaching with the focus on a holistic approach would suit Sámi education better. Then the school schedules, conception of space and idea of learning would become more similar to the typical manner of surrounding environment. The working methods at school should be developed into more pupil-centered than before and learning environments should be seen as wider than just a classroom. For example, local people and nature could be exploited in teaching remarkably more than they are today. To enhance pupils' proficiency in indigenous language, it would also be important that the language would be more visible in schools and classrooms (see Hertting & Alerby, 2009).

In this dramatization, school rituals played a significant role as well. Educational Anthropologist Christoph Wulf considers rituals as a part of the society. Rituals may have either an including or excluding role. Moreover, rituals may involve stereotypes. Rituals are social forms where social action and its manifestations produce rules and hierarchies (Wulf, 2008). Also teaching epitomizes the transmission of rituals. Rituals appear in the everyday life at school in various events and shifts and they help keeping the system together. That exact feature seems to be the primary factor that separates school from enculturation. Along with the original research, it started to seem that it was the question about a larger entity than just school arrangements, such as keeping the doors locked, teacher-led instruction, and placing desks apart. Maintaining the charade does indeed necessitate routines. School days start in a certain, repetitive way: the first lesson takes place, then a break, the second lesson, the third and so on.

Yet, this kind of school routine is not in accordance with the Sámi worldview. Nor do the Sámi have a school history of their own that would have been formed from their own starting point. School is an unfamiliar concept and institution for the Sámi: originally, it was brought to the Sámi community by outsiders, missionaries and state representatives. The tradition of Sámi education is relatively short due to together with disparital power relations which there are deficiencies at every level. Among others, these deficiencies are the constant lack of qualified teachers and cultural sensitive learning material in the Sámi language. However, the situation has improved little by little because of teacher education and learning materials provided in the Sámi language. As the Sámi do not have widely materialized self-governance, they have not been able to develop the Sámi School from their own premises.

The Reliability of the Research

Especially in qualitative research, the reliability of the research should be evaluated at each phase of the research. The research can be evaluated with four concepts: inner validity, outer validity, reliability, and objectivity or—as Lincoln and Guba (1985) further suggest concerning qualitative research—with credibility, transferability, dependability, and confirmability. The research could be evaluated through the criteria designed especially for mixed methods research. Mixed methods research can be evaluated with independence of the methods, insulation of the data, interdependence of the methods, integration, and the aim of the research (whether it is comparability or contrast) (Brewer & Hunter, 1990). Thus, the reliability of the research can be strengthened with a variety of data, researcher, or theory (Johnson & Onwuegbuzie, 2004; Lincoln & Guba, 1985) and the first option was used in the research in question – although naturally all parts of the research have to be executed carefully because mixing methods does not compensate for badly performed parts of the research.

The researcher's role should not be forgotten either: According to Michael Quinn Patton (1990), it is all about the researcher's reliability because the researcher is the ultimate instrument and the core of the analytic process. Furthermore, in school ethnography, the researcher always affects the action in a classroom with her presence to some extent. In Keskitalo's (2010) research, the teachers were asked to describe how much the researcher actually affected in the classroom in order to check the inner validity of the research. In other words, it was about the Hawthorne effect (see also Adair, 1984; Uusikylä, 1980).

It is worth noticing that if the researcher does not spend a long time at school so it could be difficult to assess the researcher's influence in the classroom in the long term. In Keskitalo's research, during the first days at school, the Hawthorne effect was evident but eventually, students got used to the researcher's presence. Some students reacted strongly while other did not react at all. The researcher's presence could bother them: it was manifested by glancing at the camcorder constantly and asking whether the camcorder was on or off. Sometimes, the researcher's presence had positive effect too as her presence could calm down the atmosphere in the classroom.

In Keskitalo's (2010) school ethnographic research, observation was participative and partly active. Especially at the children's school level, students could ask the researcher for advice and therefore, she acted as an ancillary teacher. Similarly, during breaks or playtime, students could ask the researcher to participate in playing or games. At the middle school or juvenile school level, the researcher worked mainly as an outside observer.

School ethnography is unpredictable and this feature manifested itself in this research as well. The researcher could not know beforehand how long the process would take in reality. Informing people about the research process, acquiring permissions, and recruiting the schools for the research took time before carrying out the actual research. The purpose of the research and its course were openly described at the phase of recruiting and visiting the schools. Did the teachers change the practices due to it? Although teachers would have concentrated on planning their teaching and working methods more than usually during the lessons that were observed, they would have only showed their proficiency.

Often, the time spent among the research target is evaluated in ethnographic research. However, according to Forsey (2010), the outcomes of ethnographic research should be judged more by the quality of the representation of the lived reality than with how much time one spent in living this with the persons captured in ethnographic text. In other words, too often the research is assessed according to how it was done rather than by the strength of its findings and the skill of the analysis. This was the aim of this research as well and it closely connected with the highest role of an ethnographer as the dramatizer described in the previous chapter. The reliability of the research was also strengthened by careful preparation before carrying out the observations by familiarizing with the written curriculum and research on curricula, discussing with the teachers, and becoming acquainted with the school plans and documents.

Observational research has its problems, too, because events that take place in the classroom are difficult to interpret because of their multidimensional nature. In addition, researching how the curriculum is realized in practice requires plenty of time and is laborious (Rønning, 2002). Indeed, studying the conflict of socialization at school is a many-sided target because socialization and curriculum theories are multidimensional as well (Øzerk, 2006).

It is quite typical of qualitative research that the research theme is defined, specified, and altered all the time. During the research process, many sides of the research were specified in the text and the researcher's thinking constantly. The research shaped from a fragmented one into more structured. Little by little, the researchers perceived better what the school change is eventually about. School ethnography appeared a functional means to research Sámi education and culture and to contribute to the aspirations of changing the teaching culture and classroom practices.

Discussion

Ethnography is a research process where the researcher brings forth his/her relation to power questions, ethics, and researcher's responsibility (Skeggs, 1999b). Ethnography aims at describing and understanding cultural experiences, including classroom situations. Furthermore, ethnography can be empowering because it gives space to teachers' voice (Spindler & Hammond, 2000). Revealing and contemplating the power relations are important themes in the discourse about indigenous peoples; for example, researching the limitations, order, and practices at the Sámi School. The meanings can be analyzed by conceptualizing the context where the school functions in daily life. Meanings and cultural relationships are intertwined, and thus bring out the power questions (Lehtonen, 2004/1996).

New kinds of approaches are needed to canvassing and figuring out the societal power structure. Also, James Collins (2009) argues that we have to consider multiple levels of social and institutional structure as well as microanalytic communicative processes and cultural practices in education and society with new kinds of tools. Indigenous peoples' have their own kind of knowledge, value, and ontological theories (Kuokkanen, 2000, 2007). According to Nils Oskal (2008), it is not possible to have a special and tenable methodology. Hermeneutically enriched research requires scientific humbleness, openness, and courage. Indigenous peoples' worldviews cannot be ignored either. Indigenous peoples' research should help peoples to attain self-governance through empowerment, survival, development, mobilization, changing, and decolonization (Smith, 2012).

The epistemological starting point in our research work was founded on the principles of minority research. According to these principles, everyone has knowledge of something and it is always produced in cooperation with others. The question is about various ideas of knowledge (Mohanty, 1994). From this standpoint, methodological aspects are closely connected with the information production, diversity, power relations, and paradigmatic questions (see also Eddy, 1997; Ford, 1997; Spindler, 1997; Wolcott, 1997; Wulf, 2002). In the educational-anthropological approach, the familiar is seen as unfamiliar in order to perceive the hidden meanings. In order to change things, the special characteristics of the target have to be brought out. Therefore, the original research introduced in this article aimed at describing the special features of Sámi education extensively. In addition, openness is typical of ethnography. The research is not grounded on certain hypotheses but the data is derived from cultural context. The most important task is to create a coherent idea how to raise children in a more diverse society than ever before (also Spindler & Hammond, 2000).

The concepts of transculturation and inter-culturation describe the transformation from cultures living side by side toward inter-culturalism. The diversity of the Sámi School originates in the tradition of colonization and the decolonization process that follows it. The Sámi's political awakening, *Sámi lihkadus*, and cooperation with indigenous peoples embody this awakening. Sámi communities are relatively large because of the geographical reach of their settlement. Inner, cultural, and livelihood related differences are also great; in addition, the diversity manifests itself as multilingualism. The local multiculturalism consists not only of the Sámi, Finnish, Norwegian, Swedish, and for example Kvens but also other ethnic minorities: all these languages increase the language-sociological richness in the everyday life at the Sámi School. Moreover, the political situation including legislation and human rights has to be taken into consideration. In the school context, ecological and cultural factors affect students' cognitive, affective, and social development (Seitamo, 1991).

The context of the Sámi School may be viewed through transculturation as it explains transition as the foundation of social continuity. The purpose of the Sámi School is not to homogenize culture so that the dominant culture would play the main role. Instead, heterogenization, new kind of diversity, should be emphasized. As a salient part of transculturation, the extrinsic and local are mixed and this interaction produces new re-contextualizations. Therefore, the concept of transculturation is important as it helps understanding the situations where cultures confront and proved a new perspective to the power relations and decolonization processes (Judén-Tupakka, 2003). Furthermore, in the diverse Sámi School context, it is important to be aware of the differences in experiential worlds that affect individuals' processes of adjustment, integration, and ethical diverging (Eidheim, 2007). For diversity, it is important that the Sámi School context is not simplified or categorized too radically through the emphases in the definition of Sáminess.

Ethnography can help designing an indigenous educational model that is culturally responsive, and rigorous, and supports students' success. In today's world, globalism and multi-culturalism place various challenges for education, and culturally sensitive education is one of the most important issues concerning these challenges (see also Labaree, 2003; Schoorman & Bogotch, 2010). Therefore, the education of minorities and indigenous peoples is of great importance as well because of their endangered and liminal position in the society. Research and theory are important to indigenous peoples because it helps understand reality, make hypotheses about the world where they live and, first and foremost, create strategies and control criticism toward indigenous peoples (Smith, 2012). According to Maori Researcher Kathy Irwin (1992), theory is not any academic luxury but a necessary part of revolutionary equipment. It is a tool that can harness the powers of mind, heart, and soul. Irwin thinks that indigenous peoples do not need outsiders to develop methods that would help them to understand who they are. Indigenous peoples can do it by themselves. Ethnography conducted at Sámi teaching contexts is, according to researcher Keskitalo's field work, possible through a Sámi perspective and with respect for the Sámi voice. At its best, ethnographic research can bring out indigenous peoples' voices and self-expression, and the prevailing power relations. Thus, it can affect the course of actions and strengthen Sámi people's position.

Ethical Perspectives on Sámi School Research

The research contexts of indigenous peoples and Sámi education are versatile. The diversity of the Sámi School originates in the tradition of colonization and the decolonization process that follows it. Sámi communities are relatively wide and scattered because of the geographical reach of their settlement. Inner, cultural, and livelihood-related differences are also great. In addition, the diversity manifests itself as multilingualism. Local multiculturalism consists not only of the Sámi, Finns, Norwegians, and Kvens, but also other ethnic minorities: all these languages increase the language-sociological richness in the everyday life at the Sámi School. Moreover, the political situation including legislation and human rights has to be taken into consideration. When the purpose is to rethink schooling from the perspective of indigenous peoples' own needs, it is worth asking how research, educational practices, and curriculum have to change to recognize and incorporate local forms of knowledge and ways of knowing. Along research, the importance of indigenous knowledge is being realized (Murillo, 2009)—even to the extent where methods of collecting, analyzing, and presenting data characterize the western academic tradition as well as indigenous ways of knowing, communicating and sharing knowledge (Webster & John, 2010).

Recently, more attention has been paid on how the western education has affected individuals, and local cultures and knowledge (see e.g., Barnhardt & Kawagley, 2005). In the school context, ecological and cultural factors affect students' cognitive, affective, and social development (Seitamo, 1991). Linguistic and cultural diversity provides that teaching arrangements are student-sensitive. This refers, for example, to such activities where the teacher notices students as individuals and encourages them to develop their thinking (Zahorik, 1975). This kind of collaboration turns into a communal and individual construction process of skills and knowledge enabling cultural participation.

This chapter discusses ethical challenges in Sámi education and is focused especially on research conducted in schools where members of indigenous peoples act as research partners (see e.g., Sarivaara, 2012). In this chapter, we discuss the ethical challenges of Sámi school ethnography and how to conduct ethnically sustainable research among indigenous people. Ethical viewpoints are contemplated here from the point of view of the choices and omissions made by the researcher. Special attention is paid on indigenous children as research partners. Ethical choices in Sámi education research relate to the following themes: choosing the research theme, data collection, and the research relationship between the western/indigenous researcher and indigenous research partners and between adult and child in an indigenous context. Ethnographic research necessitates a responsible role from teacher-researchers as they have to be able to notice Sámi children's and people's rights and special cultural features and to be in close collaboration with the Sámi community—on the Sámi's own initiative and terms. The specific questions that we will discuss in this chapter are what are central conditions that direct ethical choices in educational ethnographic research; how to obtain research data in an ethically sustainable manner in educational ethnographic research?; and what is the researcher's ethical responsibility when conducting ethnographic research in the Sámi classroom?

When researching school, teaching, and learning, children's rights as research partners have been strongly addressed (Alderson, 2001; Mayall, 2000). In addition, child research has its own special features that differ from adult research (Punch, 2002). Our study offers an example of negotiating and enacting ethical principles for research involving a marginalized population: children and teachers who are members of an indigenous people.

Ethical Principles of Ethnographic Research in the Indigenous Classroom

"Relevance, respect, relationships, and reciprocity are valued characteristics of ethical practice in all social research" (Ball, 2012, p. 1). Moreover, the ethicality of a research has been compared with the purpose of aiming at finding moral principles that prevent from harm and injustice and promote goodness, reliability, and honesty (Sieber, 1993). Ethicality as a concept includes, among other things, defined moral principles and dominant rules, such as autonomy, privacy, reciprocity, and equity as commonly recognized principles (see e.g., Morrow & Richards, 1996).

Thus, research on indigenous children involves numerous ethical tensions. It is especially important to notice factors that relate to the selection of the research theme (Flewitt, 2005; Ford et al., 2007), how representative a sample children in that particular study make (Hill, 1997), the autonomous space given to each child in the research (Moss & Petrie, 2002), and data collection methods and the framework for data analysis (Grover, 2004). These issues are topical and worth contemplating by researchers who are doing research among sensitive groups such as children and indigenous peoples (cf. Peltokorpi et al., 2012).

When conducting research in an indigenous classroom, a researcher has a great responsibility. He or she must not harm pupils and the surrounding indigenous community in any way (see Graue & Walsh, 1998). Indeed, ethical choices are generally accentuated in this kind of child research. In addition, children as research participants are heterogeneous when it comes to their sensitivity, skills, and learning abilities (see Boekaerts, 1995).

Ethical Questions of Sámi Research

The special terms of Sámi research

Researchers have to consider certain fundamental conditions. We divided them into three viewpoints that frame the actual implementation of ethnographic research at an indigenous school context.

Research partners' right to be proactive, and commit to and withdraw from the research

Under the title *Knocking on Heaven's Door* Marit Myrvoll (2002) described her confrontation with the question: "Will the village have me?" Likewise, "getting in" is difficult in school research. Research can also cause resistance. A researcher has to be aware about resistance power, and be prepared to solve out resistance directed to the practical research but also to the school change (Brown & Strega, 2005; Evans, 2001). In research ethics, it is common to think about individual consent. However, not only individuals but also groups may be entitled to—and need—protection. On the other hand, Anne Barron (2002) focused her contribution *Traditional Knowledge, Indigenous Culture and Intellectual Property Rights* to the discussion of intellectual property rights. Patents, copyrights, and brands are examples of legal instruments to regulate right to a certain type of knowledge but which do not seem best suited to protect indigenous rights. She discussed other possible options to protect such rights (see also Porsanger & Guttorm, 2011).

Consequently, researchers are decision-makers who choose their foci, define their methods of data collection, analyze and interpret the data, and develop plans of action based on their analysis (Mills, 2007). Naturally, the initiative can be introduced by the indigenous community as well. When a research theme is very sensitive, plenty of obstacles to participation can occur. Sensitivity in this case may mean that the study involves some questionable elements, such as issues related to intimacy, stress, and religion, or the research can bring out revealing and stigmatizing or blaming information. In such case, the sensitivity widely affects the whole research process, such as ethical choices, the recruiting of research participants, and research procedures (Powell & Smith, 2009).

The sensitivity of the research theme is connected to the agreement to participate in research. Mary Ann Powell and Anne B. Smith (2009) have argued that in most studies, ethical approval is the same as agreement but in child research the perspective has to be turned into children's participation and their assenting to it. If the research can have a traumatizing effect on the child, it may become an obstacle to the child's participation. Minimizing this assumption starts from the researcher's ethical choices that aim at increasing research participants' feeling of security and removing those factors that can possibly harm children and the indigenous people they represent.

In the research on which this chapter is based on, the researcher was a member of the Sámi people and therefore realized that she was not an outsider or neutral. In the classroom research, the researcher's own basic values were strongly present. The request for participating in the research was not directly addressed to Sámi children although, according to studies, children are fully capable of giving their own assent (cf., Fargas-Malet et al., 2010). On the other hand, the study was merely focused on the everyday practices and operation of the classroom and the researcher's task was to reflect and evaluate it. Naturally, the permission for the research was asked from the Sámi children's parents and also the school and Norsk Datatilsynet regarding the video data. Along the research process, various partners' participation and commitment to the research became a natural part of the everyday life at school. It is also worth noticing that in indigenous research, negotiations with the local community at various phases of the research are important.

Indigenous children's rights and protection

The role of ethicality is also important in ethnographic research that is carried out in the classroom by a researcher who is simultaneously a member of an indigenous people or indigenous pupils' teacher (Mills, 2007). Naturally, there is always the great danger that indigenous children are treated as a homogenous group although every child has different experiences and points of view, and they might quite well be aware of the matters in their surrounding life (see Dockett et al., 2009). The concept of rights is derived from the effect of the society and its conformance with the law. The society produces certain kinds of citizens' and children's rights which may appear in the field of social sciences so that researchers may become encouraged through more participatory approaches in their studies. As children's societal rights seemingly hint of their ethical and moral excellence, the researcher may find it difficult to regard ethnographic research with criticism (Nind, 2011).

In ethnographic research, a child is no longer a research target "possessed" by the adult but an active actor of an indigenous community. But how does this appear in practice? In the sample study of this chapter, children could participate in the actual doing and express their opinions in learning situations. Yet, the practical reality in the Sámi school world dictated the methods that a researcher could use. Is it possible to pay attention to all pupils and draw a reliable picture of everything that happens in a teaching situation? Who are being noticed through observation?

The researcher's voice inevitably is intermingled with the research because information is produced in a socio-constructivist manner. This is a typical trait of ethnographic research but one that has to be realized. Furthermore, the researcher has to be selective and choose a research theme to determine the perspective of his or her observation. Therefore, pupils and teachers could have had special attention, for example, based on their Sámi language proficiency. It is reasonable to ask how children's individuality is recognized in the research if all who are willing are not allowed to participate. Or, do we assume that some Sámi children speak for all Sámi?

The ethics in child research can be divided into three main categories: informed consent, confidentiality, and protection. Informed consent is connected to the research approaches created by adults or researchers and that respect children and treat them justly and honestly (Morrow & Richards, 1996). Furthermore, the researcher-child relationship contains various power structures—also, if indigenous perspectives are included (e.g., whether the researchers is a member of an indigenous people or not, etc.). A researcher can use his or her power to selecting techniques that allow children to feel a part of the research process (Morrow & Richards, 1996).

Research that is focused on children and Sámi people may represent a process of understanding dissimilarity. The process involves questions that relate to ethicality and those roles and tools that are used when studying select participants with the purpose of learning about the school culture. It means that the research contains various proportions of children's voices and reflection which emerges from the researcher being present in the indigenous school world.

The special nature of the Sámi culture

When it comes to Sámi research, research ethics is connected not only to general research ethics but also Sámi research policy and ethics. It means that Sámi research should, for example, benefit the Sámi society or disseminate information about Sáminess (see also Länsman, 2008). Indeed, special ethical situation- and context-based challenges embody Sámi research. Sámi theory of knowledge, perception of the world and value system can be revealed through investigation of Sámi concepts as well as through research analysis. Indigenous research can draw on all previous Indigenous and Western research and theorizing (Porsanger, 2007, 2011).

According to Tove Bull (2002), a researcher has to be familiar with the Sámi's history, traditions, culture, and language in order to be able to research the Sámi society. Ethical requirements that concern research among indigenous peoples are, for example, responsibility for disseminating information and local participation. In addition, the researcher has to respect local traditions, values, languages, people, and families. All information has to be handled in confidence. Furthermore, participants have to approve the research (Porsanger, 2007). The researcher has to be aware that he or she will meet the research participants later on as well (Nystad, 2003).

Ethically sustainable ethnographic research

It is essential that the researcher evaluates how select research methods and techniques—including methodological choices, ethical practices, and data analysis and interpretation—can bring out Sámi children's voices and draw picture of Sámi education. A researcher who studies children should choose such a data collection method that will not harm children psychologically or emotionally (Fontana & Frey, 2005; Tomal, 2003) or make children feel anxious in any way (Alderson & Morrow, 2011). Neither should the method affect the pupils' learning environment in the classroom negatively (Tomal, 2003). The researcher's fears, expectations, prejudices, and opinions on children may have an influence on methodological choices (James et al., 1998). It is possible, for example, when the question is about researching people or issues that are close to the researcher (see Young & Barrett, 2001).

In Keskitalo's (2010) research, the data were collected through a combination of methods. They were utilized to reach the special traits of the Sámi education. According to findings, multiple techniques should be employed in ethnographic research because the research phenomenon is so versatile and because they allow research participants to express themselves in various ways. Next, we will discuss three methods: observation, interviews, and a research diary.

Direct observation

One data collection method in the sample research of this chapter was direct observation. The clear advantage of it is that the researcher can acquire first-hand information. The method was chosen because it enabled the researcher to collect research data from the real-life situations which cannot be acquired from secondary sources (see also Tomal, 2003). The observation method has a long tradition in small children research (Clark, 2005).

Observation provides many-sided information as it is a combination of listening, watching, reflecting, and evaluating. Certainly, it is possible that a researcher becomes blind to some classroom phenomena—especially, if the researcher is committed and well familiar with the research field and the dominating basic values. As a member of the indigenous people, the Sámi, the researcher of our sample study had a certain standing point which could have biased her observation. Yet, her familiarity with the Sámi language and the Sámi culture made it possible to notice how such traits of the Sámi culture that would have remained unnoticed by a western researcher were included or omitted in teaching situations.

However, child observation has also its limits: What should be the relationship between a researcher who is doing the observation and the child observed? Some researchers think that adults can do research by adopting only the researcher's role because adults' and children's worlds are so different, and that age and authority hinder them to fully participate in children's world (see Goode, 1986; Mandell, 1991). Furthermore, adults are claimed to be unable to participate in children's social world because in reality they are not children ever again (Hill, 1997). Thus, it is the most crucial to critically reflect and reason the select methods and procedures and how they can be implement in research focusing on indigenous children's contexts (see also Barker & Waller, 2003; Fargas-Malett et al., 2010).

Interviews

According to Bryony Beresford (1997), interview is one of the best methods when applied in the context of daily life. In this research, Sámi teachers and pupils were supposed to express their opinions and perceptions in interviews. Interviews were to function as a support to deciphering the research theme (see also Tomal, 2003).

Interviews make it possible to a researcher to check whether his or her interpretations of the reality are equivalent with the actors he or she observed, and whether their voices were allowed to be in the center in the research text. As mentioned in the previous chapter, the fact that the researcher and children had similarities cultural backgrounds was considered an advantage. Still, when addressing children, there are certain principles that are important to the ethicality but also to the reliability of the study. For example, interview questions have to be designed in a child-friendly manner in order to be suitable for small children (see also Fargas-Malett et al., 2010).

Cultural and language differences often become a barrier between indigenous and non-indigenous populations. Therefore, interviews should be culturally appropriate and consciously decrease bias. Everyday conversations with indigenous people is one means of adopting effective techniques. Open-ended questions allow interviewees to tell their stories with minimal interruption and prompt of information by the interviewer. Ultimately, indigenous people may be better acquainted with narrative telling than they are with question-and-answer responses (Powell, 2000).

A researcher's diary

A research diary is a tool for making notes about pupils' and teachers' actions and teaching and learning practices, and overall atmosphere of the research situation. In practice, direct observation implemented in this research is a practical method that, according to Daniel R. Tomal (2003) is easily convertible into an anecdotal form. When anecdotal notes are made in the classroom, the key factor is fast observation on the important behavior which is relevant to the research (see Mills, 2007).

However, making notes or videoing during lessons may activate pupils in a particular way. Tomal (2003) warns about this: people can become motivated to perform better when being observed. Because of Hawthorne effect the researcher is encouraged to minimize participants' awareness of participating in the research and, thus, the learning environment at the Sámi School was maintained as natural as possible. A research diary complements an ethnographic study and data in many ways, helps to remember happenings in the field, and, first and foremost, functions as a means to reflect the researcher's position in the study. Indeed, research diary colors the events of the field. Research diary can be scaffolding researcher's construction of research knowledge (Engin, 2011). All the way we have to be aware that particularly qualitative research in social and cultural settings, is experienced subjectively. The quality of the data gathered is related to the quality of relationships the researcher is able to establish with informants in the field (Newbury, 2001).

A researcher's ethical responsibility in Sámi research

Sensitivity to notice events in a Sámi classroom

A researcher wishing to study Sámi education encounters a complex world that is not easy to enter. The role of an ethnography researcher involves high-level reflectivity and sensitivity. In the research described in the chapter, deep learning resulted from combining reflection and practice (Somekh, 2006). At the same time, the researcher's self-comprehension developed which is particularly important in ethnographical research because data analysis and the process of interpreting the significance of development happens through the researcher's self which also functions as the research instrument. The development of self-comprehension improved the quality of research so that the researcher began to realize how individual factors, values, and presumptions molded the research results (see also Peltokorpi et al., 2012).

In indigenous research, ethnographers have to be able to adopt several roles. First, they must pay attention to cultural sensitivity. The western school system dominates instruction in the Sámi School, and therefore students are not socialized into their own cultures in sufficient amount.

Second, the school ethnographer needs to describe otherness. Ethnography and anthropological research tradition have been criticized especially for their focus on otherness and pursue of defining primitiveness. Research subjects are described as others, exciting, and different. The concept of otherness can be changed along with the change in ethnography. In this study of Sámi education, "the other" lives in the ethnographer's experiences and is researchable, interpretable, and understandable.

Research in general and indigenous research in particular necessitates the ability to reflect on teaching events. In most educational research, reflection is defined as a useful and necessary method enhancing the critical analysis of teaching and school environment. Reflection helps researchers to demonstrate their own action, maturing, and values and to reflect on them in relation to the change (e.g., Oser et al., 1992). When researchers reflect on action profoundly and frequently, they may, in a manner of speaking, lose their grip of the core concept of the research. Therefore, reflection is a dialogue between questions and answers that researchers pose to themselves.

In ethnographic research, working in the field, in communities, is a central concept. Therefore, the ethnographer has to take over the school field. An ethnographer who researches the Sámi School has a structurally wide field to study: it includes students, teachers, text books, teaching arrangements, and the community outside the school. By focusing on the everyday life at school, it is possible to understand the daily practices and processes. The ethnographer follows the events and teaching in the classroom by observation. Yet, it is impossible to observe everything that takes place in the field. Therefore, it is important that the researcher defines the limits for analysis carefully.

The abundance of phenomena in indigenous people's education and teaching situations requires of the ethnographer the ability to pull together the various sides of school and multiculturalism. The connection between the teacher, teaching, guiding, and learning is complicated. Yet, the aim of classroom research is to perceive and analyze this connection.

Reporting the results

One side of ethicality is how truthfully a researcher reports the results (see Fontana & Frey, 2005) and how the researcher analyzes and categorizes the data as the ethnographic data are often adundant and multiformity. The researcher must present those interpretations and conclusions that the results give reason for as rigorously and sensitively as possible. Specifically, the interpretation part should be as scarce and non-speculative as possible. Deduction should be based on those facts that the research elicited. Interpreting the results is the researcher's privilege and responsibility—or even a moral demand (see Heikkilä, 2002). By describing and explaining the research in detail gives the reader an insight of the participants' original experiences and bring out actuality of the Sámi School.

Moreover, the ethnographer has to work in co-operation with the indigenous community at various phases of the research. Otherwise, it is not possible to develop indigenous education (see also Lipka et al., 1998). Research results have to be returned to the society where the study was carried out. After handing the findings to the use of teachers and schools, the researcher has redeemed one ethical principle of quality research on indigenous peoples; namely, return the findings to the use of research partners (Barron, 2002; Bull, 2002).

Discussion

Indigenous peoples have their own ways of determining what is necessary to know: they have a special understanding about the world and life. Nevertheless, not even ontology and ethics are common to all indigenous peoples. Moreover, according to Jelena Porsanger, certain basic requirements concern indigenous peoples' methodologies and research ethics. These requirements appear in the relationship between researchers and research participants, and these questions are relevant to Sámi epistemology, methodology planning, and implementation of Sámi research projects (Porsanger, 2007).

Furthermore, interaction with research partners has a salient role. In other words, it is important to build and cherish trust between the researcher and research participants. Communal participation and decision making is important when conducting research in indigenous contexts. Participants have right to be heard and informed during the process. The interaction between researcher and participants is sensitive as the researcher has to have social antennas and be aware of cultural dilemmas and clashes that are going on further in society.

Finally, we want to point out that research ethics provides clear lines of accountability and control in relation to the subsequent value for, and impact of the research on Sámi education, particularly if the research involves non-indigenous researchers (Hill & May, 2013). When the purpose is to ethically engage to different knowledge systems, knowing what a particular indigenous knowledge consists of and how it is acquired, is fundamental if one wants to be able to use the knowledge. Likewise, having all parties to be aware of the value of using the knowledge is essential (Hammersmith, 2007).

How do the Sámi Culture and School Culture Converge – or do They?

Although the school has operated in the Sámi community for centuries, the Sámi people do not have a school culture of their own being born from their own circumstances and based on their own values. This is the case although the Sámi people do have their own learning and teaching culture. Furthermore, the Sámi people do not have an educational history that would be based on their distinct circumstances and their way of thinking. Thus, the school is a foreign concept and institution imported into Sámi society by outsiders (Sara, 1987); although the historical presence of school has lasted in the area for a long time. Because of these characteristics, it could be stressed that school culture in Sámi schools is in liminality. Furthermore, cultures collide easily (Hannerz, 2003). According to Mikkel Nils Sara (2003), the reason for the estrangement of the school from Sámi culture is that there was no need for the school to be aware of and take into account how to provide culturally sensitive teaching earlier. Culturally sensitive teaching is based on the Sámi premises. The collective rights of Indigenous peoples emphasize their right to preserve and develop their societies (Henriksen et al., 2005).

This chapter examines how school supports the Sámi culture. Further, it reflects the connection between the conceptions of socialization and enculturation within the instruction at the Sámi School. In this chapter, school culture is the main concern. Stuart Hall (2003) has defined culture as the system of common meanings applied by people belonging to the same community, group or nation in order to understand how the world functions. Culture as a concept is complicated; especially, what it comes to the Sámi School as diverse ethnic groups and many languages operate there. How is the system prepared for the multiple realities? This chapter concentrates on the culturally sensitive situation within the Indigenous people's schooling system. Starting from this point, the aim of the chapter is to analyze how the school culture and the Sámi culture meet. At the same time, the question of how the school supports the Sámi culture is at the center. What is the connection between socialization and enculturation in Sámi education?

Socialization and Enculturation

Although Sámi traditional upbringing has not been in a major role in institutional education it is still at the core when addressing issues concerning Sámi education. In the 1950s, Paavo Päivänsalo (1953) studied Sámi child care and upbringing from the perspective of socialization. According to the researcher, Sámi upbringing aimed—based on the Sámi way of life—at socializing children into the Sámi society of that time. In that context, the concepts of socialization and enculturation are analogous. The goal of Sámi upbringing was to enculturate children into the prevalent culture and contemporary naturalistic Sámi environment.

The socialization and enculturation concerning the Sámi become pushed to differentiate when the mainstream cultures arrived in the Sámi area. Onward, historically, the significance of the school is based on nationalistic ideas and this has also steered its curriculum. The use of the concept "enculturation" is of current interest now as the usability of the concept for analyzing and interpreting materials and phenomena from different cultural contexts is studied (Judén-Tupakka, 2000; Wulf, 2002).

In anthropology, enculturation is often used as a synonym for socialization. However, the concepts are not completely equivalent. Socialization emphasizes becoming a member of society, while enculturation stresses becoming a member of a cultural community and adopting a culture. Thus, socialization means that one becomes socialized into society, whereas enculturation means that one adopts and internalizes a culture (Kneller, 1966; Manninen et al., 1994; Suoranta, 1999). Enculturation means the process during which an individual adopts the customs, beliefs, knowledge and ways of behavior of his/her own culture. They are learned during a lifelong process of working and living one's daily life (Manninen et al., 1994). The difference between socialization and enculturation can be that if socialization takes place without enculturation, an individual may lose his/her cultural heritage. Usually, the present education and upbringing at school aim at socializing a child into society. In the traditional culture, parents aimed at teaching a way of life and making children adapt themselves to the community through enculturation (Judén-Tupakka, 2003). Enculturation carries information about upbringing and the family values that have survived as a part of cultural heritage.

Enculturation is a process of becoming a Sámi; during which an individual adopts the beliefs, knowledge and models of behavior that are needed for acting as a member of the culture. The members of the culture are enculturated in childhood when things are practiced and learnt while performing everyday chores. Later initiation rituals and other life experiences contain elements that enhance enculturation. Enculturation steers identity formation and the development of one's self-image (Barfield, 1997).

From the Sámi point of view, enculturation and socialization steer partly the Sámi and the majority of population in opposite directions. Enculturation aims at maintaining the culture, whereas the purpose of socialization is to adapt the Sámi to the dominant society for example through the school. The culture and way of life of the dominant society still today are sometimes quite different from the Sámi ones, and this is something that people have traditionally become used to and adapted to in the Sámi area. The traditional Sámi world-view and way of living deviate from the present ones to a great extent. One needs to respect and maintain traditions and roots but also adapt oneself to society and its tempo. Enculturation and socialization conflict when they do not have a joint sphere of activity. It is crucial to maintain and show respect towards the Sámi heritage both by the mainstream culture and the Sámi.

According to Eeva-Liisa Rasmus (2004), enculturation is crucial for Sámi culture: through enculturation, young Sámi people acquire a strong Sámi identity preventing them from assimilating into the dominant population. Peter S. Sindell's (1997) study showed certain irregularities in the enculturation of Cree Nation of Mistissini children during their first experiences of school. When children begin school, they have to start following other norms than the ones they are used to. Furthermore, they have to exert knowledge that is foreign to them, and communicate in a strange language in an unfamiliar environment (Sindell, 1997). Such experiences are shared by the Sámi as well. Today, however, most Sámi children have been in contact with the mainstream language and culture before starting school and therefore their situation is not the same any longer at that broadness. They also have gotten possibilities to learn the Sámi language in various ways. Still, there are for example similarities in how unfamiliar knowledge is handled, often unconsciously. Nevertheless, the situation is different. As a result of colonization, the Sámi have lost parts of their cultural heritage. Hence, one of the challenges is to reclaim the norms and conceptions of knowledge that are distinctly Sámi. For example, enculturation into the livelihoods of a Sámi family and the socialization at school may conflict with each other. If young people are to learn the Sámi way of life and the tasks it involves, the young need to participate in the activities of the nature-based economy although these activities are not determined by the holiday schedule or thinking, worldview, and values of the basic school ideology. This is when enculturation at home and socialization at school can clash.

The most crucial question is how Sámi heritage could be maintained within the school. The issue has to be covered comprehensively in order to chart the whole Sámi field. At the present moment, the Sámi do not have recent common education policy conformed to nowadays situation, as the Saami Council drew up its policy program in 1989 including education (see Sámiráđđi, 1989). Indeed, the Sámi people need to adapt themselves to the dominant society but how: through assimilation or integration? From this point of view, it seems important to examine the concepts of enculturation and socialization. For Sámi education, it is necessary to reflect on how to reconcile the issues of the past, present and future. This way of thinking is in line with Jerome Bruner's (1963) ideas on the spiral curriculum. Analyzing the relationship between education and upbringing at home has mainly focused on the conceptual meaning of enculturation and the emic approach (Lauhamaa et al., 2006). These two constitute a part of epistemological understanding, the sphere of living, and view of the cultural context.

The Western School Culture Dominates

The data showed that the ways of the western school dominate instruction in the Sámi education.

> *The timetables were divided into 45-minute periods and the school day was organized by the time allocation. Time allocation defining the minimum number of lessons for core subjects.* (Research Diary 2001, 2006, 2007)
> *The lessons consisted mainly of filling in the text books.* (Research Diary 2001)

The problem in many Sámi schools is that their pedagogical arrangements and curricula are similar to mainstream schools.

> *In the morning, when arriving at school, the pupils come in the school after the school bell has gone. They hang their outdoor clothes on the racks situated outside the classroom. After this, the teacher opens the classroom room with the key. At the classroom, the pupils stand at their desks and say good morning in unison before they sit down. They listen to the teacher's teaching and start working with their text books. After the 45-minute lesson, the pupils go for a 15-minute break. The subjects changes into some other one after this. This pattern is repeated day after day and week after week, month after month, and I suppose also in other years too.* (Research Diary at the children's school level, fall 2001)
> *There is not just one well-designed series of text books for Sámi primary education but I have to look for the best parts that support the goals of a subject from a variety of books.* (An interview at the children's school level, Teacher no. 10, spring 2007)

The Sámi School is organized based on the prevailing values. Rather than skills and attitudes, it is affected by the values of one kind of information society. The problem of situation of Sámi language appears so that the visual environment at the schools was scarce. Neither the pupils' Sámi language nor themes that emerged from the local culture functioned as stimuli. Sámi language did not get visibility as the linguistic sociological situation would demand.

> *After observing the notice boards, I noticed that the language used in announcements was Norwegian language. It clearly breaches the Language Act and the principle of equality.* (Research Diary at the children's school level, middle school level, and youngster's school level, fall 2001)

According to the findings, Sámi culture and school culture do not meet in an appropriate manner nor is the Sámi School very sensitive culturally. The school does not notice the special characteristics of Sámi culture sufficiently. Of the countries that have a Sámi population, the Sámi people's rights come true the best in Norway. Yet, Sámi schools still are as if in the middle ground between western and Sámi schooling: they are Sámi schools governed by western school culture and pedagogies (see also Hollins, 2008).

How to Organize Sámi Education: The Sámi Conceptions of Time, Place, and Knowledge

The problem of the school is that it cannot solve the ways how teaching is arranged in the western school world referring, for example, to teacher-centered teaching which is tied to text books. Subject and time allocation epitomizes this kind of the teaching arrangement as well. Organizing teaching with the focus on a holistic approach would suit Sámi education better. Then the school schedules, conception of space and idea of learning would become more similar to the typical manner of surrounding environment. The working methods at school should be developed into more pupil-centered than before and learning environments should be seen as wider than just a classroom. For example, local people and nature could be exploited in teaching remarkably more than they are today. The study focuses precisely on the encounter between formal and informal learning. Therefore, we need to have a look at the Sámi conceptions of space, and the nature and society-based understanding of place (Hoëm, 1995) and of time and knowledge (Helander & Kailo, 1999). In this context, mediating structures have a central role and their purpose is to alleviate the cultural conflict (Nurmi & Kontiainen, 1995).

Figure 2 illustrates enculturation and socialization through mediating structures. The western style of organizing teaching in school system can be seen to bringing Sámi pupils apart still partly from being Sámi people as the school interprets the values of western world. Therefore, it is important to break the organizing ways of teaching familiar to the western school system.

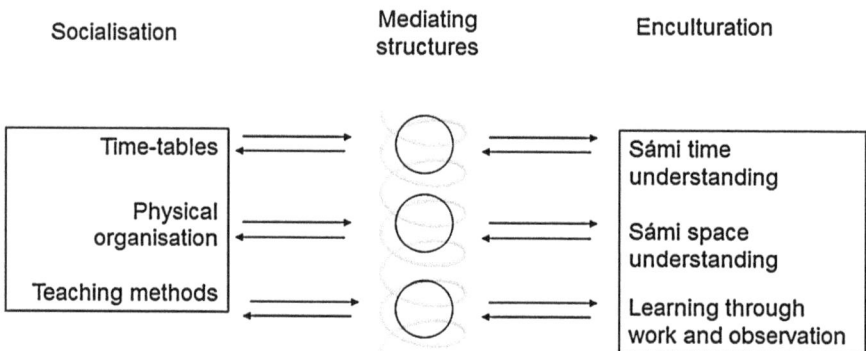

Fig. 2. The mediating structure of Sámi education

Time allocation, classrooms, and working methods have to be re-organized. For this re-organization, Sámi conception of time, place, and knowledge are important. The purpose of the hermeneutic circle is to form entities where history, present situation, and future are combined in education. It is a philosophical conclusion that could solve the main problem of school in practice: how to become a true Sámi School at the present time and place, in this moment and now. It is remarkable how time, place, and knowledge are understood and organized at school. Smith (2012) writes that the place of Indigenous peoples is colonized. At the mainstream culture, place is usually understood for example architecturally but in Indigenous peoples' conception place includes people and quite intangible levels as well. It can be stated that Indigenous peoples are obliged to have, for example, the spatial conception of place typical of the western countries. Similarly, school participates in molding for pupils the conception of time that represents initially foreign culture with no connection to the tradition with yearly sense of time. The same can be said of knowledge: at school, the authority holds the information and thus it is not formed together, which would be suitable and typical of the traditional Sámi culture.

It is necessary that the time allocation at school, the form of classrooms, and working methods are reconsidered. It would be natural to cut loose from the time allocation and think more widely than just classrooms. In addition, the working methods should be more and more pupil-centered. The present form of school should be conceived all over again. Then, it could fit the Sámi situation better than the prevailing form does. Although Sámi upbringing has not been in a major role in institutional education, it still is at the core when addressing issues concerning Sámi education. Solutions for the organization of teaching at the Sámi School and its problems can be searched in informal upbringing. Thus, the basis of teaching could have a comprehensively socio-constructive (Piaget, 1978/1977; Vygotsky, 1976) and ecological approaches (Ogbu, 1988; Sarason, 1971; Seitamo, 1991).

Discussion

According to Paulo Freire (2006/1970), education always handles power relations and the achievement of objectives. Training includes a fundamentally arbitrary cultural system, which is based on an invisible power relationship. Recreating culture through education seems to play a key role in the reproduction of a complete social system (Althusser, 1970; Bourdieu & Passeron, 1990). In this process, the school is a socially conservative force (Bourdieu, 1977). It means that education becomes the central terrain where power and politics operate in the lived culture, in the asymmetrical political and social positions of individuals and groups. Education should be seen as a type of counterforce for the colonization of the mind and the heart. To arrive at decolonized pedagogy, we need to take seriously, on the one hand, the interplay between knowledge and learning and, on the other hand, the experiences of the students and the teacher. It is essential to theorize about and politicize the experiences, if pedagogic measures focus only on systemizing leadership and on the assumptions of disciplinary knowledge. We need to take into account pluralism: uncolonized pedagogical measures require that we pay serious attention to various types of cultural logics, as they are fitted into asymmetrical power relations (Mohanty, 1994).

From the point of view of Sámi culture, enculturation is a challenge especially because the Sámi curriculum and its implementations in instruction do not enculturate pupils into Sámi culture in the sufficient level. Through strengthening mediating structures, it might be possible to succeed better with micro-level instruction and learning than nowadays in the multiple learning contexts. The Sámi worldview and Sámi values should occupy a central position in teaching but also in curriculum. Teaching should be organized according to the principles of open learning environments at the Sámi School.

Culture is transferred through upbringing and education. Learning can be formal taking place in the traditional way at school or informal happening outside the school (Goetz & LeCompte, 1984; Judén-Tupakka, 2000, 2003). Cultures do not provide their members with a finished operational model: they are more like processes (Huttunen et al., 2005). It means that culture is not an innate characteristic but created in a range of ways through experiences and interaction (Kvernmo & Stordal, 1991). The Sámi School should pay attention to this perception and, therefore, school cannot be handled like static, ready organization in diverse situations, but as an organ in a burgeoning position.

Sámi life contains a great deal of informal knowledge. This knowledge is holistic and place-bound; it is also an important element in socialization. Taking this approach into account gives children and young people better skills to encounter the modern world (Bergland, 2001). There are also differences in worldviews; for example, the imagery in the world of the Sámi drums depict life as being divided into three levels (see Westman & Utsi, 1998). Knowledge that is based on science holds a dominant position in the school—which is right. The problematic thing is that this knowledge is abstract and not connected to the daily life. After all, everyday life is concrete and based on daily experiences. School should pay attention to pupils' own experiences and establish the learning into these premises pedagogically.

In the Sámi context, schooling has been criticized from the collision perspective (Hoëm, 1978; Høgmo, 1989). In addition to power issues, the short tradition of Sámi teaching results in deficiencies at all levels. These shortages introduce the continuous lack of competent teachers in Sámi language as well as culture-sensitive teaching material. However, the situation has gradually improved as a result of Sámi teacher training and the production of teaching material in Sámi. As the self-determination of the Sámi has not been realized comprehensively, the community cannot develop the school on its own terms. In addition, we talk about a school culture, which cannot, as such, fulfill the needs of the Sámi.

Toward the Practical Framework of Sámi Education

Our previous chapters have already shown that the special features of Sámi education are not considered in teaching arrangements sufficiently. Education at Sámi schools is not culturally sensitive enough and it should be further developed. Culturally sensitive school notices the important role of the local culture and its worldview and values when it comes to teaching arrangements. In this chapter, our purpose is to present a practical framework that opens, and therefore highlights the factors that enhance such teaching practices that help confronting and supporting Sámi culture in instruction and school.

In this chapter, we concentrate on the culturally sensitive situation and cultural-historical background factors within the indigenous people's schooling system and discuss the encounter between different cultures. Sámi School in Norway is heterogeneous because diverse ethnic groups and many languages operate there. We will analyze and describe how well the system is prepared for the reality, and what kind of special features it has; and what should be taken into account when pursuing acting in a way that pays attention to the situation in the field of the manifold school.

The Development of Sámi Education

In Scandinavia, curriculum development was connected to church until the very recent years. In Norway, the curricula that came into operation in 1858 and 1890 in elementary school defined the guidelines of teaching that had to be completed locally (Gundem, 1990). The elementary school curriculum of 1939 emphasized working methods and student activities so that pupils' own qualifications would be at the core of teaching. The 1939 curriculum defined the minimal level of teaching making the implementation of pedagogical contents more difficult (Hiim & Hippe, 1998). The life cycles of the curricula of Norwegian comprehensive school have become shorter. The curriculum of 1939 was effective for 35 years between 1939 and 1974. Mønsterplanen (1974) was used between 1974 and 1987 (13 years), Mønsterplanen (1987) between 1987 and 1997 (ten years) and Læreplanen (1997) between 1997 and 2006 (nine years). Norwegian national curriculum Kunnskapsløftet and Sámi curriculum Máhttolokten took effect in 2006-2007 (Øzerk, 2006). A separate Sámi School was established simultaneously with the Sámi curriculum in 1997. The Sámi School is a school which follows the principles of the Sámi curriculum in the district area of the Sámi language in Norway.

Promising Models for Indigenous Peoples' Education

Some indigenous peoples have been able to develop their schooling conditions since the 1970's. The Maoris' education in New-Zealand gives an encouraging example. They have implemented self-government that also covers education. The Maori have also developed their own Kaupapa Maori educational philosophy that is applied at schools (Bishop & Glynn, 1999; Macfarlane, 2004; Smith 2003). Kaupapa Maori pedagogy is a manifestation of power relations within the context with an indigenous people. Kaupapa Maori pedagogy is firstly based on the idea that the indigenous peoples' right to self-government is at the core of practical goals and teaching contents. It concerns every educational sector. Important are also the position of the local culture as the foundation for teaching, the communal nature of knowledge, the detection of socio-economic and family-related factors, noticing the concept of extended family and relatives in the society as well as appreciating the collective vision and philosophy (Bishop & Glynn, 1999).

Also in Alaska, about forty years ago, Yup'ik Inuit started developing their school culture when a group of indigenous teachers began the work in collaboration with the university personnel (Lipka et al., 1998). In this project, the teachers developed teaching strategies so that they would take into account students' cultural experiences, local values, communicative norms and communication styles in a better way. The idea was to become aware and simultaneously pursue breaking out the western teacher's role that the academic teacher education departments model. These behavioral models are for example voice control that comes from the western culture as well as controlling the teaching and the way of acting as an authority. These teaching elements are culture-bound (Nelson-Barber & Dull, 1998). The resultant from the development project was that more attention was paid to Yup'ik culture, social organization and the change in the routines of classroom discourse, the development of culturally understandable pedagogy and paradigmatic change of research (Lipka & Yanez, 1998).

The Practical Framework of Sámi Education

Based on Keskitalo's (2010) research, we created the practical framework for Sámi education (see *Figure 3*). In this framework, Sámi education is based on consideration certain outer and inner factors that mold the practical framework for Sámi education. Based on these factors, the practice, implementation, research, and theory of Sámi education can be advanced.

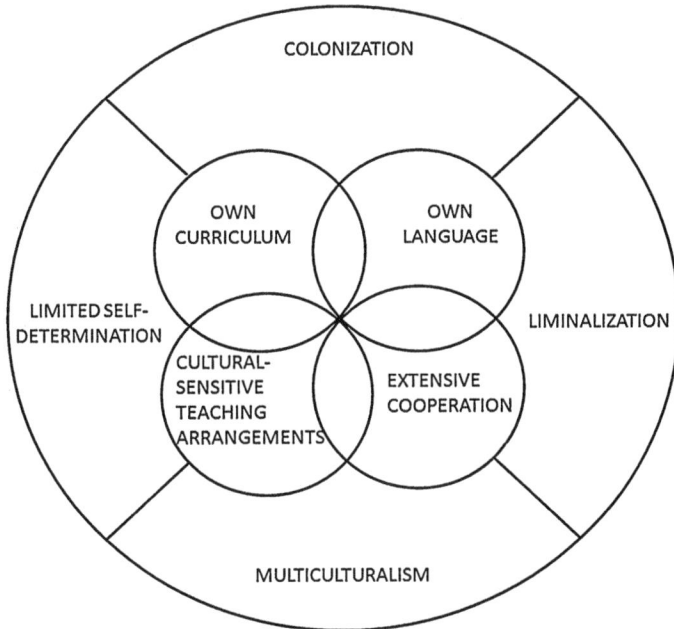

Fig. 3. The practical framework of Sámi education

Wider outer factors are reflected in Sámi education providing a background for the implementation of education. Sámi education is colored by *colonization*, acts in a *liminal* position or in interfaces, acts in the field of *multiculturalism*, and acts within *limited self-determination*.

The following four inner factors are at the core of developing Sámi education. Not only they advance Sámi education but are also salient for developing indigenous peoples' education in general: creating the indigenous peoples' *own curriculum* based on own values and knowledge system, strengthening the position of the indigenous peoples' *own language*, creating *cultural-sensitive teaching arrangements*, and diversifying the *extensive cooperation*.

The background factors

When developing Sámi education, it is important to realize what kind of cultural-historical phases it is premised on. These background phenomena are fundamental factors that form the background or merely a historically-determined burden to the independent formation of Sámi education. In the outer base, the role of Sámi education could be considered the instrument of colonization, liminalization, multiculturalism, and limited self-determination.

Sámi education is colored by colonization
In addition to church, the school system has a significant role in the colonization of indigenous peoples. A central process in the relationship between the arctic and sub-arctic indigenous peoples and formal education is the one how the arctic indigenous peoples have become subordinated by the western culture and education. Because education causes change, it can be assumed that the western culture has affected the indigenous peoples' societies regionally in quite a similar way. Certain regions have been within the ambit of western education already for 300 years while others only for forty years (Darnell & Hoëm, 1996). The genesis of the Sámi standard language and the very first books written in the Sámi language are connected to the Reformation as well (see Capdeville, 2009).

The Sámi school culture has been molded according to the outer bases. There are not any models of Sámi schools where the influence of colonization could not be recognized. The colonization of the Sámi means that the people were finally divided within four countries because of the nations' sovereignty and thus, the national states started governing the Sámi's life. Little by little, the self-determination of the Sámi's own polity, the Sámi village system, *siida*, disappeared. The Nordic colonialism was, indeed, supposed to end after the Sámi would be assimilated. The idea about otherness lies behind colonialism justifying the subordination of indigenous peoples: otherness has determined the relations between indigenous peoples and nations until today. The aim of colonialism was also to govern the region in order to make economic use of the area by using its nature. Furthermore, colonialism causes indigenous peoples' social inferiority in relation to the dominant population (Eriksen, 2007). The counter process of colonialism is decolonization which is closely connected with the concept of self-determination (Dehyle & Swisher, 1997). Decolonization refers to a long-term process that involves tearing down the administrative, cultural, linguistic, and psychological colonialist power (Smith, 2012).

Sámi education acts in a liminal position or interfaces
Given the colonized school history of the Sámi School and the influence of the western school culture, it can be stated that Sámi education and research function on a variety of frontiers. They can be seen both as physical and mental frontiers (cf. Anzaldúa, 1999). The position on the frontiers is concretized in many ways. When the question is about geographical borders, the practical pedagogy of Sámi education, both the tradition of western upbringing and science of education and the indigenous people's rearing culture, can be seen in the operation on the frontiers. The cultures have certain languages, codes, and dressing that people assimilate. The question is whether the school culture is similar with one pupils have become used with at home, whether pupils make themselves at

home when at school or whether they consider it odd and yearn for a more familiar environment, whether different things are valued at home than at school.

The Sámi live in four countries and therefore, they have to follow teaching practices from four different countries. In the research data (Keskitalo, 2010), it manifested itself for example in using Sámi text books from various countries in teaching and the problems and challenges that occurred because of it on practical teaching level.

These kinds of problems originate in the fact that the learning and teaching of the Sámi language has not been studied at the pupil level thoroughly and comprehensively yet. However, processes which are focused on deconstructing knowledge about Sámi language instruction spring up in the educational field (see e.g. Myrvoll, 2005; also Aro, 2009). On the other hand, also the reasons that come from the language sociology of the Sámi language have an influence as the situation of the language is weaker than the situation of the dominant language, Norwegian. Therefore, teachers can be blind to the power of the dominant language in teaching and do not necessarily know how or are not getting enough support to handle the situation. The blindness of teachers and the school system can be explained with the colonialist processes. Also the power of dominant western school culture can prevent the school change.

The task of the school has changed as the school history proves. The previous segregating, excluding, and assimilating education directed to the Sámi has been replaced by integrating education. Instead of assimilating learners to the societal practices, teachers should guide them to break the boundaries related to, for example, social class, gender, or ethnicity (hooks, 1994). The task of the school has changed also globally as the industrial society has developed into information society. The increasing understanding about the challenges of diversity increases the need for analyzing the content of education and knowledge. Awareness of the threatening factors of colonization and globalization affects in the background.

The Sámi School in the field of multiculturalism

Due to its starting point, the Sámi School is not a coherent concept. At the ideological level, it represents a radical view of multicultural school: at the Sámi School, there are pupils who are Sámi as their ethnic background but others as well. The various ethnical backgrounds of the pupils and personnel at some municipalities and schools may have caused uncertainty of how the multicultural school with diverse values could be executed.

Because of multiculturalism and the fast changes in modern demands and learning contents, the school has to renew its practices constantly. The old practices do not work in the changing and diversifying work any longer. On the other hand, the Sámi culture has reached a transitional period which poses the danger of losing the traditional skills and knowledge. This point of view places challenges for Sámi schools.

According to Aimo Aikio, who has gotten acquainted with the Sámi life policy, the solution to changing the Sámi School into multiculturalism requires the realization of cultural and linguistic equality. The minority language has to have power and everyone in a multicultural society should be polyglot and receptive to multiculturalism (Aikio, 2003). Changing the power relations is the key word: The Sámi should have more power to follow through their own education and determine their own curriculum.

Sámi education acts within limited self-determination
The Sámi's educational self-determination is realized insufficiently from the modern point of view. The lack of self-determination leads to the situation where the Sámi do not have much control over the macro-level framework of education. The Sámi's real participation in national curriculum planning and defining the standards is limited. The phase and extent in which the Sámi have been able to affect the planning of Sámi education in reality has been criticized. Vuokko Hirvonen and Asta Balto emphasize that just the demand to be heard is not enough if authorities and decision-makers do not take into consideration the results of these hearings in their final decisions. Keeping quiet about things is structural violence that nations have practiced against their own minorities and indigenous peoples for a long time they note further (Hirvonen & Balto, 2008). Giving the Sámi self-determination concerning education would require political effort and becoming more aware of the matter than before also in education.

In order to undergo a transformation, Sámi education has to be considered as one of the factors that construct a welfare state. Although self-determination in education is restricted at the moment and self-government has not yet come true on a large scale, the legacy of assimilation should be turned into a new kind of future with decolonization (e.g. Smith, 2012) and empowerment (e.g. Bishop & Glynn, 1999).

The inner factors

Developing the practices of Sámi education necessitates renewing the implementation of teaching and paying attention to the inner action that takes place in classrooms and at schools. The quality of teaching depends decidedly on how the Sámi succeeds in creating pedagogy that leans on Sámi culture. Then, it is important to develop own curriculum, strengthen the position of own language, create cultural-sensitive teaching arrangements, and diversify the extensive cooperation. All this aims at improving the indigenous people's overall wellbeing and equality.

Developing the Sámi's own curriculum

A curriculum supports teaching in functional indigenous peoples' education by having indigenous peoples' culture, knowledge, and information in the center. This kind of curriculum which combines the indigenous people's knowledge and western way of thinking should be developed in active cooperation with the indigenous people's community. The curriculum should provide such a learning environment, teaching activity, and didactics that it not bound to a specific subject. This kind of content and meaning is outlined through the cultural-sensitive teaching arrangements.

The central and extensive features of the curriculum could be respect and appreciation of the Sámi's own and other cultures. These principles are salient features of intercultural education. Inter-culturalism derives from the need to establish rigorous and respectful dialogues between different forms of thinking and knowledge stemming from indigenous peoples and western experiences in such a manner that makes it possible to come up with a synthesis of the way of thinking, which in turn can be approached and acted upon (see Chacón et al., 2010). The most important goal is to increase understanding, tolerance, and solidarity between various groups. People who are not members of indigenous peoples should be encouraged to have a positive attitude toward indigenous peoples' language and culture. Further, the Maoris in Aotearoa emphasize "the Maori for all" perspective which aims at getting the Maori culture and language an equal position in the society and usable as cultural capital.

In addition, the diversity and cultural value of the learning materials that are included in the curriculum should be paid attention to. Learners and community members should participate actively in curriculum development which grounds on the indigenous peoples' cultural identity and history (King & Schiermann, 2004). For example, in Central America, local actors and university staff have produced cultural-sensitive learning material in a cooperation project (e.g. Programa de educación intercultural multilingüe de Centroamerica, 2008a, 2008b). According to Odora Hoppers (2002), the individuals and communities of indigenous peoples – the personal and organizational level – should be empowered. Educational culture that leans on learners' cultural and experiential strength would make both pupils and their parents as well as teachers understand themselves, their culture, and others' cultures, too (Macfarlane, 2004). These kinds of follow-throughs have been implemented in Nordic Countries; for example, learning materials in the Sámi language are produced. However, these matters have to be further developed to avoid the problem of translating the western material directly into the Sámi language without adjusting the material to the Sámi culture. Assimilating procedures at school, such as culturally unadjusted learning materials, should not remain unexposed.

The Sámi curriculum should form the stone base of educational development. Thus, the curriculum would lay the foundation for supporting cultural sensitivity and cultural diversity. Teachers should have more responsibility, integrity, and autonomy to have better conditions for changing teaching. Traditional teachers' pedagogical skills are not enough in multicultural classes because the everyday happenings that take place in them are so versatile. Teachers' capacity to adopt the new role calls for supplementary education. Therefore, a variety of issues concern school, education, and curriculum planning: educational policy, Sámi policy, school culture, and teachers' role.

The Sámi curriculum and school activities should be adjusted with the surrounding cultural, economic, and geographical factors. It is important the northern school systems would adjust to the changing conditions in circumpolar regions (Darnell & Hoëm, 1996). In this kind of pedagogy, pupils would be taught such skills, attitudes, and knowledge with which they can succeed. In addition, flexibility is important for avoiding overloading the goals and contents of the curriculum. Multicultural learning environment is challenging.

Strengthening the Sámi language

Well-functioning education of indigenous peoples also advances the indigenous peoples' language usage simultaneously supporting the proficiency of national and international languages. According to the ideology of multilingualism, language is not only a communication tool but also a central cultural element. Although the Sámi already realize Sámi language teaching in quite a successful manner compared to many other indigenous peoples, there are still nuances that should be re-thought. As a whole, teaching and learning should be implemented in the indigenous people's language at every school level, and it should also include the indigenous peoples' fund of knowledge in the curriculum. Learning material in indigenous peoples' language should be produced and tested locally and the whole teaching and especially teaching reading skills should focus on the indigenous children's own language at the initial phase of education. It enables moving on to learning other languages progressively and in a culturally suitable manner that notices the learners' own needs and starting points. Native speakers of indigenous peoples' languages should be hired as teachers. Learning other languages is considered supporting intercultural understanding and tolerance (King & Schiermann, 2004).

Securing the teaching and learning of Sámi language with all its teaching arrangements requires time, the development of didactics for reading and writing the Sámi language, creating a functional model of bilingualism and cutting down other arrangements related to the school system. Language revitalization programs and strategies must be brought to schools and the society in general. Although the necessity of using the indigenous peoples' languages and the importance of multicultural programs were recognized in teaching, a variety of problems may occur. Firstly, there is lack of literary learning material written in indigenous peoples' languages. Also, the number of monolingual teachers slows down the positive development. Pupils' parents can still be afraid because of their previous experiences that their children will not learn the dominant language well enough and therefore, they do not offer their children the opportunity to educate themselves in the indigenous peoples' languages (King & Schiermann, 2004). There are still many practices in Sámi teaching which should be examined in relation to the language sociological background.

Cultural sensitive teaching arrangements
In order to make Sámi education cultural-sensitive, it has to perceive the meaning of the socialization task of the school organization. Therefore, it should also be considered what kind of cultural wellbeing Sámi education constructs. In Tara Yosso's model communal and cultural wellbeing is created through aspirational, familial, social, navigational, resistant, and linguistic capital. Aspirational capital means the ability to maintain hope and dreams concerning the future even when confronting obstacles. Familial capital is defined through cultural knowledge and through it communal and cultural memory, history, and intuition have been transmitted from one generation to another. Social capital includes the net between people and communal resources. Navigational capital refers to tactical skills for coping with various social institutions. Resistant capital consists of knowledge and skills that can be used for challenging inequality in the light of equality. Linguistic capital emphasizes intellectual and social skills that have been learned by using many languages (Yosso, 2006).

This model of cultural wellbeing can enhance cultural-sensitive teaching where the question is about the power relations between various groups of people. The cultural and linguistic reality at school has to be taken into consideration (see Bailey et al., 2008). Within the cultural localization and possibilities provided by diversity, people's own language and culture should form the foundation for all education (Spivak, 1993). Schedules, physical spaces, and working methods are important if we want to develop teaching (e.g. Cuban, 1993).

Indigenous peoples' way of thinking can be considered consisting of values and worldview. The challenge is how to take the connection with nature and local society into consideration within study units. Indigenous peoples also emphasize the meaning of experience, and social and holistic views when acquiring information. In these cases, knowledge is derived directly from the environment where people live. Furthermore, highlighting criticality and power relations is seen extremely important. When describing the core elements of Sámi fund of knowledge, Helander and Kailo stress that knowledge itself does not have any goal but utility value. People participate directly in producing and sharing knowledge. The epistemological truth comes forward through stories, conversations, negotiations, and evaluations on the activities that have taken place as well as recalled memories and experiences. In addition, knowledge is tested in various real-life and working situations. All this happens without scientific formal action (Helander & Kailo, 1999). When applied in the school context, it means that knowledge is not considered something occupied by authorities but shared.

Community-centered school work

Educational principles and working methods, that are based on the indigenous people's culture and traditions and that are developed in cooperation between the institutional education and the indigenous people's community, are offered as the solution. Then, education would be linked with every area of life, pupils' wellbeing as well as the environment and land. The foundation of indigenous people's communal opinion, value, goal, and aspiration should be noticed in order to be able to together decide what, when, and why pupils should learn something. Hearing the community members, parents and the elders, is a method that helps recognizing traditional upbringing practices and working methods (King & Schiermann, 2004).

Developing the school is an all-round happening that concerns the whole personnel and pupils as well as requires cooperation with families, the community and society. Comprehensive development helps and supports teachers' work. Teachers' efficient work demands inner motivation and engagement to the class and the school. External change in the administrative structures does not solely guarantee efficient learning; nor does just the reconstruction of education change the way of working at the classroom. The new kind of thinking and new working methods have to be adopted before action can change for good. The change takes place as teachers' pedagogical skills develop. Teachers' mastery over the subject contents, pedagogical thinking and action are important when the goal is to improve the efficiency of teaching. To guarantee the quality of teaching, the focus has to be on the improvement of an individual teacher's skills and motivation; but at the same time, the inner structures of school have to be developed so that they support good teaching. The shared value basis at school and mutual support among the personnel are crucial factors.

Teacher education should support the growth and development of teacherhood toward the new kind of teacherhood where teachers become guides or cultural mentors in learning situations instead of taking the teacher-centered role. It means changing the school and learning culture. Furthermore, teachers' in-service and post-graduate education has to be developed. The form of present teacher education could prepare students better to implement teaching in a way the curriculum requires. It would be necessary to make sure in teachers' basic education that teachers have the skills, attitudes, social background, and motivation needed as well as the ability to act as a teacher in the rapidly changing world. Education and the change in attitudes are the key words.

Discussion

Because of the historical processes in the regions with Sámi population and the position that the Sámi have in relation to the national states, the Sámi teaching has been long marginalized outside the influence channels and possibilities. In addition, the nowadays Sámi School is not yet independent as it is also burdened by the governing power hierarchies. The need for power relation and paradigmatic change is included in the further development of Sámi education. Because of the power arrangement of the Sámi School, it would be necessary to solve the macro-level problems first in order to make the micro level work better than it does today.

Academic-based knowledge holds, and certainly should hold, a dominant position at school. What is problematic is that this kind of knowledge is unconnected with everyday life and thus abstract as well. Yet, everyday life is concrete and based on the daily experiences. It is also problematic if the society and nature do not sufficiently participate in the everyday life at school. The hybrid theory as a part of sociological theories (e.g. Lowe, 2005/2003) could explain this matter in the indigenous peoples' situation because it considers the society, nature, and culture hybrids as interconnected. At the same time, the hybrid theory pursues solving the societal participation by explaining an individual's part in it. The hybrid theory supports the diversity of the Sámi School because it accepts Sámi education. According to the theory, communication is important and natural premises offer several possibilities for it. One extremely salient issue is the language-sociological situation that varies, in this case, by families and individuals: the age when the Sámi language is learned and the levels of knowledge of the Sámi language may vary. The hybrid theory could also explain how the Sámi language is learned and thus, the task of the society and school would be to support this process, not to prevent it. Hybrid could also mean that various system start working in networks. Establishing a network between the Sámi education and its surrounding society is the most topical issue.

A View on Sámi Language Teaching

Vitality of indigenous languages is directly proportional to the vitality of biological diversity. "The disappearance of species of plants, animals, or insects and the destruction of an ecosystem means the disappearance of related languages and knowledge" (Tauli-Corpuz, 2009, p. 6). Linguistic diversity is being threatened around the world and this threat is acutely felt by indigenous peoples. The survival and development of indigenous languages will require the will and efforts of indigenous peoples as well as the implementation of supportive policy, especially in the field of education (United Nations Permanent Forum on Indigenous Issues, 2008). Therefore it is important to scientifically discuss the position of indigenous languages in teaching.

Language is the way to a profound cultural understanding: it is a central part of teaching and provides valuable cultural information and a world-view that pupils can find significant (Hall, 2003). The purpose of this chapter is to describe the North Sámi language instruction at the Sámi School of Norway and Sámi classes in Finland through these questions: what is the state of Sámi language instruction in compulsory education?; what kinds of teaching methods and learning materials are used to teach the Sámi language?; and how is pupils' background taken into consideration in compulsory education in Norway and in Finland?

The Realization of Teaching in the Sámi Language

The state of Sámi language instruction in compulsory education

It seems that language teaching has area- and country-specific differences although there are plenty of in common as well. Overall, large-scale language revitalization has been possible in Norway already for a longer period of time. The aspiration is to increase the number of active Sámi speakers. Indeed, it is a political goal that is agreed at the state and municipal level.

According to observations and teacher interviews, teaching in the Sámi language functions more and more like language immersion in Finland—yet a bit differently from what an immersion course traditionally refers to, namely, as a means of revitalization. This is because the Finnish school system does not know the principles of language revitalization as widely as the Norwegian one: in Finland, the schools are Finnish while in Norway, there are Sámi schools. This is quite a practical difference between these two countries. There is need in Finland also to bilingual solutions as there are more pupils who would need options to get the Sámi language back if it is lost during the assimilation. Though, it is not possible in every municipality in Sámi home district, because some municipalities have accepted only pupils with Sámi as their first language in Sámi language classes. Some of the classes are composed of native Sámi-speaking pupils and those who have passive knowledge of the Sámi language when they start school. Teaching in the Sámi language can be compared to language immersion because instruction has to be adjusted to resemble an immersion course due to the pupils' various linguistic backgrounds. Some pupils may have not had the chance to go to a Sámi-speaking day care before going to school.

The principle of inclusion, Sámi curriculum for all, has been in use in the Sámi administrative district of Norway since 1997. Thus, it has a 15-year-long tradition at the municipal level. According to the principle of inclusion, pupils who belong to other ethnic groups or come from various linguistic backgrounds also attend Sámi language classes, especially in some municipalities in Norway. Due to research data similar individual examples were also found in Finland.

Currently, three types of Sámi schools and models for using and studying the Sámi language exist in Norway: (1) Norwegian-speaking schools where the Sámi language is studied as the second language, (2) Sámi-speaking schools, or (3) bilingual schools with Sámi and bilingual classes. All these schools follow the Sámi curriculum and the Norwegian school system works separately outside the Sámi language administrative district. In Finland, there are municipality-level Sámi and Finnish classes in Sámi domicile area.

In Norway, pupils study many languages starting from the first grade which takes time from the teaching and studying of mother tongue. In Finland, pupils at the elementary school at first grades study basicly the subject of mother tongue approximately 6-7 hours per week while in Norway they have 3.5 hours. In Sámi classes, there are at least six hours Sámi language and an hour Finnish language teaching in Finland at first grades.

At the moment, Finland has a revitalization plan consultation for Sámi languages going on, and Norway introduced a Sámi languages action plan in 2009. Nonetheless, the municipalities seem to lack an efficient language policy that would protect the Sámi languages. Furthermore, the lack of an ideology that emphasizes language planning in a general level is a central problem in the context of Sámi languages. However, resources for revitalizing the Sámi language are increasingly needed.

According to the research data, learning to read and write was considered the most important in Finland. This is mostly because of historical reasons: in Finland, the most salient aim when constructing the young nationhood in the beginning of the 20th century was to educate the Finns with emphasis on literacy.

Starting from the very first day at school, pupils start working diligently with reading and writing. They work hours every day with their own reading and writing exercises. (Research Diary, fall 2007, Finland)

According to the observations in Norway, pupils' own efforts in learning to read and write were not that high:

> *Teachers read to the pupils much in different connections during the day. However, the reading situations lacked dialogue in some cases: the pupils did not discuss the themes that were read nor did they write much by themselves. The reading situations took place mostly when the pupils had their lunch and could not take part in reading and writing situations actively.* (Research Diary, fall 2001, Norway)
>
> *Teaching seemed mainly teacher-led and textbook-oriented, and addressed social aspects instead of allocating time for the teaching of pupils' native language, Sámi.* (Research Diary, fall 2001, spring, 2007, fall, 2007, Norway; Video data, fall 2001, Norway)

Teaching methods and learning materials in the Sámi language teaching

The current era seems to call for new ways of seeing and thinking teaching; this was manifested in the data. Alongside the mainly teacher-practices, new ideas seemed to slowly take root in education. When analyzing the learning environment at the Sámi schools and language immersion, it is important to pay attention to theme and project work central in the Sámi curriculum in Norway. They are working methods that motivate pupils and their learning process and thus can help indigenous pupils, too. Various teaching methods that depart from textbook- and teacher-led teaching tradition could help pupils' language learning. Curriculum texts try to cover optional teaching methods and they have emphasis on play, theme, and project work in Norway. The practical realizations vary and the content of the Sámi School is just about to be shaped as its history is so short. Yet, the teachers who were interviewed in this study told that the Sámi curriculum was a natural continuum for the Norway's Sámi policy. In Finland, the situation is different because all schools must follow the national Finnish core curriculum.

In Norway, from the first to fourth grades, themes are emphasized in teaching while project teaching is preferred in upper grades where the subject division is more emphasized. The emphases are called a pyramid principle, and in O97S curriculum, they were defined as the foundation for the core curriculum and the local curriculum. Theme teaching means organizing the teaching content so that teaching becomes comprehensive and the content interconnected. The theme can be wide or narrow and can concern only one subject or be inter-subject. The theme is planned for a certain period, similar to project teaching.

The difference between theme and project teaching is that theme teaching resembles so-called integrating comprehensive teaching, which is the most recommended teaching method for the children's school level. Project teaching focuses on the problem-based teaching entity. This method is recommended for the youngsters' school level (grades 8-10). At the children's school level (grades 1-4), time has to be spared for play and organized teaching. The goal of a child-centered curriculum is integrating teaching that combines subject-specific teaching with theme and project work (Kinos, 2002). The purpose of theme and project teaching has been to turn teaching practices into more pupil-centered.

According to the data in Norway, teachers used theme work diversely. Twenty-two percent of the teachers reported that they used the method daily, and 36 % used it once a week. Theme work was not a common work method for everyone: 7 % said they used the method only once in a half year, and 1 % of the teachers never use it. The teachers' skills, knowledge, and experiences on theme work varied (Keskitalo, 2010). Furthermore, the teachers understood theme work in different ways and could lack knowledge about the method although it is emphasized in the curriculum:

I have thought of using more theme teaching. I think that I haven't worked as a teacher so long, and it might be an unfamiliar method; I don't know the method. Now, I may have gotten better [insight], I have familiarized myself with the method and viewed it from various perspectives. I have been given year plans from elsewhere that are planned according to theme teaching, and I have asked about theme teaching from other colleagues. (Teacher No. 4, Interview at the children's school level, fall 2001, Norway)

The second practical issue based on the data seemed to be that the problem has been deciding in what language certain school subjects should be taught and in what language the learning materials should be produced. The observational data shows that many schools use Norwegian text books when teaching in the Sámi language. The observation data from Norway showed that in many schools teachers use Norwegian textbooks when teaching in the Sámi language:

Math, science, and English textbooks are in the Norwegian language when teaching at many schools. Some schools are more conscious and use textbooks written in the Sámi language if available. In this case, the schools would even adapt textbooks from Finland; whereas other schools prefer learning materials in the Norwegian language. (Research Diary, fall 2001, spring 2007, fall 2007, Norway)

Instead of teaching in the dominant language, more attention should be paid to concepts and their development within the Sámi language. First, teaching may have taken place in Norwegian or Finnish by using Norwegian or Finnish textbooks because the Sámi language does not have settled corresponding modern concepts or teachers or pupils are not familiar with them according to the interview data. The scientific vocabulary in the Sámi language is young and teachers in this study recognized the need for developing concepts for pedagogical use, and having the Sámi community use them. In addition, from the pedagogical point of view, concepts are important for pupils' own conceptual understanding— however, the schools do not have enough resources to address this difficult situation and therefore, teachers prefer textbooks written in the mainstream language instead of linguistically difficult one in Sámi though. This kind of solution is an action which is not helpful what it comes to Sámi language situation's improvement in society, and pupils' ability in Sámi language. The following excerpt reveals that the teachers were very much aware of the situation:

> *We should work with the concepts. First and foremost, it would be important to use mathematical concepts in the Sámi language.* (Teacher no. 8, the secondary level, fall 2007, Norway)

Lack of certain textbooks was evident in both countries. On the other hand, some teachers in Norway reported using math books from Finland and did not see any problem at the curriculum level:

> *I use math textbooks from Finland in my teaching. The contents are similar to the contents of our curriculum.* (Teacher no. 9, the children's school level, spring 2008, Norway)

Although there are textbooks available for almost every school subject, they are not all appropriate and usable. Some of the books are pedagogically old-fashioned or direct translations from the dominant language without any culturally-relevant application.

It seems that it is not that easy for teachers either to stick to the Sámi language: teaching situations are complex and multiculturalism gives an extra challenge, school culture and time allocation dictate teaching methods to a large extent, there is the shortage of teaching material in the Sámi language and the textbooks could be outmoded. Thus, teachers may not be ready to such large-scale changes that language revitalization would necessitate. Some of them did not even see the value of indigenous language immersion.

Indeed, the disparity regarding the Sámi language appeared in this research when the teachers prepared the school-specific curriculum, the local application, only in Norwegian:

> *Teachers' meeting: The teachers are preparing the local school-specific curriculum for the Sámi-speaking school in the Norwegian language although they spoke Sámi in the meeting.* (Research Diary, fall 2001, Norway)

The situation revealed concretely how the teachers understood the utility value of the Sámi language or the importance of using the Sámi language. In the Finnish data, the situation manifested as follows:

> *The Sámi-speaking pupils' communication and playing language is in danger of changing into Finnish because the linguistic environment is usually*

> *Finnish-speaking. Sámi-speaking pupils tend to use Finnish during breaks being an example of how the Finnish language dominates.* (Research Diary, fall 2008, Finland)

The prevailing opinions on the value of the Sámi language are not totally up-to-date because of the history with assimilation. One interview with a teacher illustrated how the Norwegian language is chosen as a teaching language at the children's school level for example in math; or they would, at least, choose a Norwegian text book as the Sámi language would not have any utility value later on.

> *Pupils have to be able to study math in the Norwegian language later on at the youngsters' school level and that is why we have chosen Norwegian as teaching language partly and a text book in Norwegian language at the children's school level.* (An interview at the children's school level, Teacher no. 11, fall 2001)

Thus, the reason for choosing a Norwegian text book was not only explained by the shortage of teaching material in the Sámi language as the text books could be old as well. These viewpoints are paradoxical from the point of view of pupils' concept development and their knowledge of the Sámi language; it is not in line with the modern idea of multilingualism either.

> *It would be necessary to bring out what kind of conceptual arsenal pupils should have at many levels. We should work more with the concepts; that is my opinion as a long-term teacher. As far as I know, this is a problematic theme.* (An interview at the children's school level, Teacher no. 3, fall 2007)

In those schools that had selected a Norwegian text book for teaching in the Sámi language and where teaching partly took place in the Norwegian language the decisions cannot be affected or opposed if the problem is not realized. Based on the data, the decisions are usually made by the school principals. Therefore, the discussion about the teaching and text book language should be brought up at many levels. Still, the existing Máhttolokten curriculum leaves the decision to the school level. This matter should be noticed at many levels: in teacher education, educational policy, and decision-making bodies.

> *I have not been able to decide the language in the math learning material because the principal made the decision for us.* (An interview at the children's school level, Teacher no. 4, fall 2001)

The teachers emphasized the importance of strong linguistic environment for supporting pupils' linguistic talents. To be able to support pupils' linguistic talents, pedagogical expertise is important at school.

> *We have a strong Sámi-speaking environment here. The children went to Sámi-speaking day care before school. Therefore, they have quite a good vocabulary and know the concepts well. The school has the pedagogical expertise and, on the other hand, we still need pedagogical support in these*

questions. We also invest in spoken language so that children with different linguistic backgrounds can practice speaking. (An interview at the children's school level, Teacher no. 10, spring 2007)

Heterogeneous pupil groups and the gate-keeper phenomenon

Third, it was dissected how pupils' backgrounds were taken into consideration in Sámi teaching. According to the interviews, teachers paid attention to pupils' differences concerning their various linguistic backgrounds. In the interviews, the teachers said that pupils differed from each other in their Sámi language proficiency when they started school regarding their backgrounds, and that pupils learned the Sámi language at different paces:

We pay attention to pupils who do not know the Sámi language or who lack writing skills or who do not speak the Sámi language. (Teacher no. 3, the children's school level, fall 2007, Norway)

Some of the pupils already read both languages when starting school. It is a pupil-specific matter. For example, if the family has supported a pupil's learning to read. Or they have been speaking Sámi at home. If not, then we have to support these children at school. (Teacher no. 19, the children's school level, spring 2007, Finland)

These matters are observed in teaching arrangements many ways, and teachers have many strategies for supporting pupils who have started school with passive language skills:

After having explained something in the Sámi language, I can quickly translate it into Norwegian to certain pupils. (Teacher no. 9, the children's school level, spring 2007, Norway)

Both Finnish and Norwegian teachers also observed pupils' development conscientiously. Some teachers had ways of testing pupils' language learning:

I suggest that the pupils draw according to my dictation: Draw a blue house on the hill. Draw a blue snowmobile in the middle of the hill. Draw a red crow outside the house. (Teacher no. 19, the children's school level, spring 2007, Finland)

We have an agreement with pupils that we do not speak Norwegian aloud in order not to change the language of the group during lessons. A pupil may come and whisper to me in Norwegian. Pupils will not bother whispering for a long time but, in a manner of speaking, make themselves speak Sámi aloud. (Teacher no. 14, the children's school level, fall 2006, Norway)

Not all teachers used translation as their method but some of them spoke the Sámi language all the time with their pupils. Repeating and using expressions and words that children use and understand helps children to understand the Sámi language:

> *I saw how a child dared to say a number in Sámi, and it seemed that it is the start when he/she said the number again and again in the Sámi language within an hour – as many times as she considered being enough. She started to glow in a specific way.* (Research Diary, the children's school level, fall 2006, Finland)

However, these integrations were not always successful as the pupils or parents could get frustrated and could change the teaching language or school:

> *In the field, I heard about and witnessed these cases when the resumption of the Sámi language does not go easily after all. For example, either parents or teachers have decided for one reason or another to move the child away from teaching carried out in the Sámi language; usually, because of the factors related to success, motivation or amusement at school. In Finland, some children were even denied to have Sámi-speaking teaching because of their linguistic background.* (Research Diary, fall 2006-fall 2007, Finland and Norway)

Parents, teachers, and the system function as gatekeepers for teaching the Sámi language and determine whether the revitalization of pupils' Sámi language is enabled or not. In some cases, a pupil's language revitalization as the means of redressing assimilation was hindered. Mostly, the teachers, however, talked about positive events and that the renaissance of the Sámi language is taking place in many ways:

> *I saw that the child's identity became evident when she dared to start speaking Sámi.* (Teacher no. 9, the children's school level, spring 2007, Norway)

In all, teachers in this study said that pupils have changed during the last decade:

> *Pupils' proficiency in the Sámi language is more heterogeneous than before. On the other hand, the situation of the Sámi language has improved because of the changes in the law.* (Teacher no. 15, the children's school level, spring 2007, Finland)

On the other hand, not every parent had the skills to support their children because of their insufficient knowledge of the Sámi language while some parents were not able to support their children's education because the parents have to work hard to make a living:

> *If parents are farmers, reindeer herders, or entrepreneurs, they do not necessarily have time for their children. A book is not the most central thing in every family. You cannot find books on the bookshelf nor do children see their parents reading books actively. We are aware of these problems at school.* (Teacher no. 3, the children's school level, fall 2007, Norway)

Indeed, the divergence of pupils' backgrounds was described in the interviews: some parents supported pupils' schoolwork while some of the families needed support from school. In addition to cultural factors, the reason is partly the assimilation of the Sámi because some of the parents have lost their language and even their cultural identity because of lack of support during the assimilation processes.

Some parents are, however, more conscious and expect much of the school. This attitude demonstrates the change in values: Education and Sáminess are considered more and more valuable. Many expectations and much value-related pressure are aimed at the school. Many kinds of emotions are affecting to school:

The school is more valuable than before because some parents expect a lot of it. Some of the parents are conscious while some are not and then we try to convince them the importance of Sámi language learning or importance of academic knowledge. (Teacher no. 3, the children's school level, spring 2007, Norway)

The influence of Western society on families appeared powerful, and thus, the goal of the schools is, on the one hand, to maintain the traditional Sámi upbringing and, on the other hand, to bring back nature and culture as the children's learning environment:

We have to teach pupils and give reasons why they have to learn. (Teacher no. 5, the children's school level, fall 2007, Norway)

The interviews illustrated the pressure applied to Sámi schools. Schools have to decolonize their practices, families, and pupils and simultaneously academize some families

The Roundup Pen of the Sámi Language Teaching

The results showed that there are differences between Finland and Norway on how they arrange Sámi education. Norway has the conditions, the framework, to realize Sámi education but in practice, the problems are similar to ones in Finland. Despite the Sámi curriculum in Norway the actual teaching has its deficiencies. Sámi schools in Norway are in the borderline of Norwegian and Sámi schooling: they are Sámi schools but they are controlled by western school culture and doctrines. However, the idea of inclusion agreed in Norway makes language revitalization acts possible—this difference is worth noticing.

The situation of the Sámi language teaching is challenging. Although teachers do remarkably important work, their time goes with sociolinguistic and power questions leaving little time and resources for developmental work. The Sámi School does not have advanced self-determination but the definitive decisions are made by the Norwegian ministry. Self-determination comes true through separate Sámi curriculum, and local applications and implementations. Regardless of this and actually because of this, teaching should be developed so that sociolinguistic problems would be at the core and to be solved. Due to research data sociolinguistic problems are not managed to solve out in general level. The same concerns power questions and they should be discussed within communities: who has the power to decide how to develop Sámi language education. School boards or administration is not always informed—and even if they were, the school culture may hinder the development. It is so stable that giving up strict pedagogical models appears impossible even if leaning on Sámi thinking would be beneficial and make Sámi language learning and teaching meaningful. According to our interpretations, there are many different challenges in Sámi language teaching. These challenges originate in the language sociological state of the Sámi language and Sámi culture combined with the harsh background of a history of assimilation. Additionally, the asymmetric power relationships affect schooling. Children's language proficiency is influenced by different things in their background. At this phase, teaching is aimed at the beginning years of compulsory education: it simultaneously functions as language immersion for children who have passive knowledge of the Sámi language and as native language instruction for native speakers. Teachers have multiple ways of succeeding in challenging situations when trying to notice every individual and his or her personal learning processes. All in all, language planning is needed to make teaching more successful in the indigenous peoples' context: the position of the indigenous language and a culture-based approach should be adopted at the core of teaching and language planning. Teaching is organized differently in countries with Sámi populations also due to the educational history, societal differences, and the political situation. Finland has followed the German educational school system (Paksuniemi, 2009), and Norway the Danish-American system. All these abovementioned factors are illustrated in *Figure 4* which puts together findings from Keskitalo's (2010) research in Norway and her follow-up research in Finland. It presents tools that must be taken into account in Sámi education. The model presented in *Figure 4* is a reindeer roundup pen. In the center of the pen, reindeer are divided into slaughter animals and breeders. All reindeer are counted in this churn. Around the churn, there are so-called bureaus, one for each body of reindeer herders. Bureaus have a dominating position in relation to the other sections of the round-up pen. The path to the churn is a sort of delta or channel via which the reindeer enter the roundup pen.

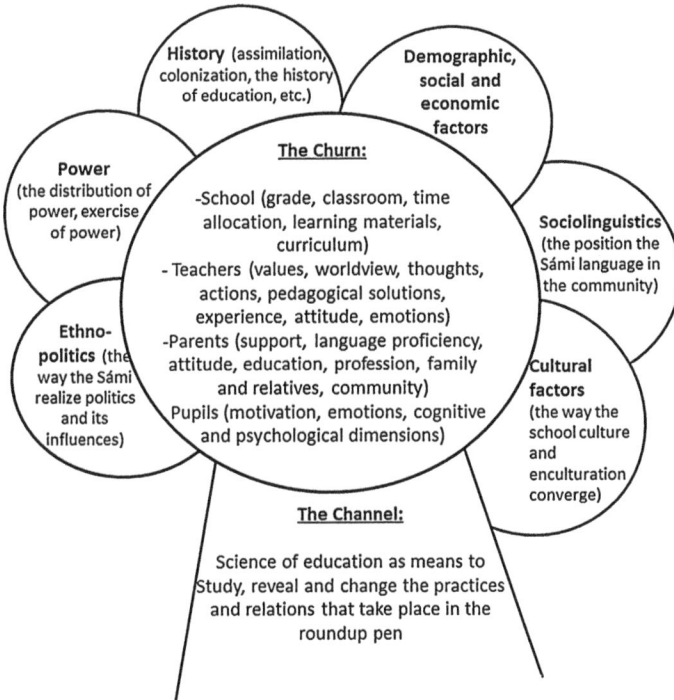

Fig. 4. The roundup pen of the Sámi language teaching

In this model, parts of the roundup pen are in subordinate positions in consummate with other parts. The bureaus represent the macro-level factors that affect Sámi language teaching. The macro level covers the background factors: there are historical factors (assimilation, colonization, the history of education, and local histories at country, municipal, and individual levels), power structures (the distribution of power, exercise of power), ethnopolitics (the way the Sámi realize politics and its influences), demographical, social and economic reasons (how and where Sámi education is supported), and sociolinguistics which is manifested in the position the Sámi language has in the community. Furthermore, there are cultural factors that refer to the way the school culture and enculturation converge.

The micro level, the churn, covers the school (grade, classroom, time allocation, learning materials, curriculum), parents (support, language proficiency, attitude, education, profession, family and relatives, community, locality), pupils (motivation, emotions, cognitive and psychological dimensions), and teachers (values, worldview, thoughts, actions, pedagogical solutions, experience, attitude, emotions).

The churn is the subordinate of the bureaus. However, it is worth noticing the channel. We consider it the way of having access to the roundup pen: science, in this case especially the science of education, has the possibility to study, reveal and change the practices and relations that take place in the roundup pen and what the connection between the churn and the bureaus is. The model is adjustable to any indigenous peoples' educational settings when the aim is to contemplate various factors that affect teaching.

Discussion

Based on the findings, it seemed that Sámi language teaching lacked a functional idea of multilingualism (see also Høier, 2007). Some issues must be focused on if we want to be successful in revitalization efforts. First, revitalization of Sámi language is not emphasized at the curriculum or practical level sufficiently. Therefore, systematic co-operation between researchers and teachers should be increased to improve the quality of the instruction. According to Kamil Øzerk (2010), Sámi language proficiency should be set, and then the language will have an instrumental value at every level of teaching as the goals (see also Kroskrity & Field, 2009). For example, in many revitalization programs in the United States, an important factor in the success of language revitalization efforts has been community members' ideas about the language, including the social meaning the speakers attach to their language and the accepted roles of using the language in the native culture (Loether, 2009). This notion is important. Indeed, Angela Creese and Adrian Blackledge (2010) have argued that flexible bilingualism can be used by teachers as an instructional strategy to show and create links between the pupils and the social, cultural, community, and linguistic domains of their lives. Because the national curricula do not support pupils linguistically as learners of the target language in language immersion, more research-based suggestions are needed (Lyster, 1999).

According to the original research, Sámi language teaching could resemble a variation of language immersion. This idea should be further considered as various language immersion methods and language nest solutions could enhance the revitalization of the Sámi languages. Language immersion is a teaching method where the target language is consciously used in a child's environment, usually at a school or day care center. For instance, various subjects can be taught with the target language at school (Creese & Blackledge, 2010; Rodgers, 2006).

The Linguistic Special Features of the Sámi Education

Curriculum as a research target forms a multifaceted and multidimensional phenomenon (Turunen, 2008). The relationship between the official, implemented, and experienced curricula (Goodlad et al., 1979) is a focal target of this review. Namely, the aim of this chapter is to analyze the special characteristics of North Sámi language instruction at the first school grades. At the same time, the question of how the school supports the Sámi culture is at the center: how the reading and writing of North Sámi language are taught at school?

North Sámi Language Instruction

The municipal language programs

The challenging nature of the language-sociological situation of Sámi language is shown in the data by the relatively heavily-built municipal language programs in Norwegian Sámi school system. Those models were adopted from the national models that emphasize the importance of the Norwegian and English languages. This kind of model is, however, somewhat unsuitable for Sámi schools as they do not pay attention to the special status of the Sámi language.

The pupils start studying the Sámi language at the first grade in the municipalities of the administrative district of the Sámi language at the same time with the Norwegian and English language in age of six. In addition, Kven-speaking or Finnish-speaking or other immigrants start also studying their own language. An option is also to study in bilingual class. (Research Diary, fall 2001)

In Norway, there is a nation-wide thought that the Norwegian language is a small language in the European context and therefore, it is important to start studying for example English early – simultaneously with the studies of Norwegian and Sámi languages. However, this educational-political definition is laborious for the Sámi-speaking pupils in Sámi schools because most of them study Sámi as their first language. Certainly, the municipality can decide on its language-political definition but the data in this research showed that there are schools where pupils study Sámi, Norwegian, and English starting from the first grade. It produces, for example, confusion with the vowels of the Sámi and Norwegian languages because in these languages the vowels 'o' and 'u' are different:

The pupils confuse the vowels o and u with the ones of the Norwegian language. (An interview at children's school level, Teacher no. 9, Spring 2007)

The municipalities seemed to lack language policy that would protect the Sámi language. An ideology that would have emphasis on language planning is, yet, a central deprivation in the context of the Sámi language. Language planning should take cognizance of the factors related, for example, to the learning of the language, the revitalization of the language, legislation processes, and cultural diversity. Language planning should be based on language policy and notice the context where the situation of the language has been charted (Bakmand, 2000). The time allocation at the Sámi schools was contemplated in the research diary:

Why do they allocate so little hours for teaching Sámi language, the pupils' native language? Would it not be important that as much resources as possible would be reserved for it? (Research Diary, fall 2007)

A demanding language program and the low number of lessons of native language combined with plenty of playing may be one reason why the pupils perform poorly in writing and reading tests. In Norway, for example, Marit Kjærnsli et al. (2007) have written about these tests. Furthermore, weak school achievements can be partly explained by the cultural clash (e.g. Ogbu, 1992). At the same time, Norwegian students enjoy themselves at school (Ahonen, 2008).

They seem to have a lot of time to mess around and sit at their own desks instead of working and advancing their language proficiency in many different ways. (Research Diary, fall 2001, fall, 2007; Video data, fall 2001)

The emphasis on reading and writing

In a letter-learning situation, pupils went through letters that were learned the last year in Norwegian Sámi school classroom at first grades. According to the data, this kind of rehearsing seems to be an established practice in the Norwegian school system when teaching the Sámi language and thus quite a problematic feature (see also Myrvoll, 2005):

The second-graders have a Sámi lesson. The theme is letter s that is rehearsed from the last year. One first-grader studies with another teacher. The teacher stands next to the blackboard and tells that they will be working aloud with the sound s. The children go and write the letters s and S on the blackboard. After that, the teacher writes other familiar letters on the blackboard. (Video data at the children's school level, fall 2001)

They only rehearsed the letters and went through the issue the same way in the first and second grade. The pupils did not get enough learning stimuli; in other words, they did not go through the whole process of learning how to read (see Lerkkanen, 2003). What is noteworthy is that unfamiliar diphthongs and meaningless words were used which – given the primary school pupils' linguistic lev-

el and the situation of the Sámi language – can be considered challenging for pupils and even confusing for their learning process:
> *The teacher writes diphthongs that do not belong to the Sámi language and meaningless words on the board.* (Video data at the children's school level, fall 2001)

According to the observation, less time is used for practicing writing.
> *Teaching is mainly teacher-led and text book-oriented.* (Research Diary, fall 2001, spring, 2007, fall, 2007; Video data, fall 2001)

According to the data, teaching the Sámi language seems to be based on learning the letters during the first grades. This educational matter is brought up here because, as mentioned before, other areas of teaching reading should also be used comprehensively.
> *Teachers used the materials made partly in Norway and Finland to the appropriate extent and saving the resources. However, the result is a patchwork because the material used is partly old and includes mechanical tasks.*
> (Research Diary, fall, 2007)

For example, Finland has got the accordant with the newest letter designs also in Sámi instruction. In practice, it makes the Scandinavian co-operation with text books more difficult because in Norway there is no letter de-sign accordance, so the Norwegian Sámi text books are only limitedly usable or adjustable in Finland and vice versa. The letter forms and shapes are not standardized in the same way in Norway as they are in Finland. The difference between Sámi education in Norway and basic education in Finland is that standardized letter designs are used in Finland: lettering and penmanship. In Finland, use plenty of time is used for combining penmanship letters so that every pupil will develop a clear writing that later on will turn into everyone's own personal handwriting. Teaching is not restricted at the first and second grades but it goes on at grades three to nine as well (Krokfors et al., 2008).

> *It is somewhat unclear whether they use lower case letters or upper case letters when teaching writing in Norway.* (Research Diary at the children's school level, fall 2001)

> *It is a teacher's choice what kind of letters he/she teaches with.* (An interview at the children's school level, Teacher no. 3, fall 2007)

Each text book producer and teacher in Norway can decide by themselves which handwriting design they will use in Sámi education. Not only makes the non-standardized letter design in Norway the inter-Scandinavian co-operation with text books more difficult but also the development of Sámi teaching because the resources are wasted in following the objectives of two states.

The order of teaching the letters

According to observations, the order by which the letters are taught varied at first grades. Based on these notions, it was important to find out what the most common letters in the Sámi language are but this information was not available. This kind of information is, however, available about the Finnish language: for example, Erkki Pääkkönen's (1990) research on the alphabet of the Finnish standard language. The language technology project of the Sámi language was asked to count what the most common letters of the Sámi language are. The electronic text collection of the Norwegian Sámi parliament consisted of 59 723 513 signs that cover the articles of Min Áigi –newspaper published in northern Sámi language between 1997 and 2006 (34 929 211 signs), the documents of Sámi parliament in Norway and Finnmark municipality between 1994 and 2008 (15 210 691 signs), the New Testament and parts of the Old Testament (1 458 935 signs), some legal texts (2 063 647 signs), six belletristic texts (1 677 479 signs), and nonfiction texts (Sámi school history, notices from the hospital of Tromsø, texts in the O97S curriculum, etc., 4 383 550 signs) (Sámi giellatekno, 2008). A, i, e, and o were the most common vowels and t, d, l, and s were the most common consonants. The order is in North Sámi language: a, i, e, t, o, d, l, s, u, á, n, g, v, r, m, h, k, j, b š, p, č, đ, f, ž, c, ŋ, z (Keskitalo, 2010, p. 163).

For example, the order in Helena Valkeapää's (1986) ABC-book is the following: a, á, i, l, u, n, o, e, s, m, d, g, b, r, h, t, j, p, v, k, c, č, š, d. The ABC-book follows the emphasis on vowels as the most common letters in the Sámi language has. The difference between Valkeapää's order and the grapheme prevalence discovered by Sámi giellatekno is, for example, introducing the vowel á already at an early phase in Valkeapää's text book. It seems important to present the difference between vowels á and a in early stage in order to make sure pupils will differentiate them. Further there is also meaning of dialect. Differences in dialects make the learning of literacy complicated. In North Sámi language, dialectic differences make it more difficult to write Sámi. The standard language is a compromise when it comes to the North Sámi language.

According to research data in Finland and Norway the order of letters presented to pupils and also the order in text books varies greatly. This phenomenon should be further investigated through systematic analysis of textbooks about letter orders compared to Sámi giellatekno order.

When producing text books, the order of introducing the letters should be contemplated based on the knowledge on the grapheme prevalence in the northern Sámi language and teachers' experiences on teaching:

According to my experience, when a pupil knows about eight letters and recognizes the same number of vowels, he/she will learn to read. (An interview at the children's school level, Teacher no. 3, fall 2007)

Marja-Kristiina Lerkkanen (2003) presents the parallel in her dissertation according to which, on average, pupils learn to read when they know ten letters. In the data of this research, letter-oriented teaching seems to be highlighted. Therefore, the order in which the letters are introduced and other issues related to it was discussed. Along with teaching reading skills, every sectors of linguistic awareness should be developed and not just concentrate on the phonological awareness. Then, the other areas of linguistic awareness are in danger even though the phonological awareness is a salient factor when children learn to read (see Valkonen & Vilska, 2002). Especially, at the second grade, repeating the letters is not enough any longer but the development of linguistic awareness should proceed towards the next steps.

It is important that pupils would realize the sound-letter congruence: it is a precondition for learning (Lerkkanen, 2003). They need thousands of repetitions and practices for noticing and learning the congruence, approximately 15 to 20 minutes a day. Based on the observation data in Norway, Sámi education does not seem to fulfill this task because the pupils did not work much with writing, reading and other tasks that would improve these skills. This seems to be also value question; whether the literacy is highly valued or not. In Finland they put lots of efforts to development of literacy while in Norway to social action. In classroom level it could be realized so that the Finnish Sámi pupils work a hard by themselves. It is obvious also that they follow academic Norwegian studies of reading acquisition, while it would be more practical to follow Finnish studies as Finnish language is a cognate language to Sámi whereas Norwegian is not.

Discussion

The linguistic challenges in Sámi education are manifold. The results illustrate the phenomenon of multilingualism related to teaching in the Sámi language. The phenomenon is understood in a variety of ways. In some municipalities, the development of teaching in the Sámi language progresses in a good direction but at the political level, the revitalization programs of the language are missing. Being almost a direct copy of the Norwegian curriculum with Sámi addition and application, the Sámi curriculum poses extra challenges for teaching in Sámi language because it does not take into account the context of the Sámi language sufficiently. The Norwegian language is the dominant language and its language-sociological context is in a state (see Todal, 2002). That is not the case with the Sámi language: The literary culture in the Sámi language is relatively minimal in comparison with the mainstream cultures and the support from media is weak. Teachers' awareness has to be improved and methods that are suitable for teaching the Sámi language have to be developed. Furthermore, it is necessary to support and continue to develop and elevate the Sámi's own educational system. Realizing the luminal phase of Sámi education is primarily important for carrying on the development work.

The language-sociological situation of the Sámi language can be described by adapting Hyltenstam et al.'s (1999) scale as a threatened language. There is no Nordic Sámi literary medium. Ávvir, a Sámi newspaper, appear five days a week in Norway. One juvenile magazine appears in the Sámi language. The news is broadcast on television weekdays and Sámi radio programs are broadcast on weekdays as well. Juvenile and children's programs are broadcast both on radio and television approximately once a week changeable amount. The role of the books written in the Sámi language is significant and therefore, it is important to find out how much youngsters and children read these books, what language the library serves with and whether the Sámi books are at hand as well as the book written in the dominant language, what is the number of the books in Sámi language the library has and where these books are located at the library: Is the language visually brought up for all or does the Sámi section situate in the best place?

The situation of the Sámi language teaching varies at schools: at some schools, the whole teaching takes place in Sámi, whereas at other schools, part of the teaching and learning materials are in the Norwegian language. Reform pedagogy may solve the problem of the lack of learning materials; pupils could prepare materials by themselves. There are also bilingual schools and at some schools, teaching is in the Norwegian language. Families have to choose between the above-mentioned options if possible due to local base solutions. At some schools, the whole personnel do not know Sámi language and therefore, they do not necessarily understand the Sámi-speaking children's native language and cultural background which is not to children's advantage. The whole study path from day care to higher education should be available in the Sámi language. In Sámi language administrative district in Norway this is realized best while outside the district there are challenges. Children's language-sociological situation varies at homes as well as among the important elements for the Sámi such as among the relatives, leisure activities, hobbies, church, and friends. Indeed, interesting questions concern the language that the circle of friends uses: What do children do in the evenings, what kind of company they are in, and what language do they communicate with? Internet and other social media are also important: in what language the services of social media are available, and in what language the children and youngsters use these media? New technology has got multiple challenges when it comes to the Sámi language.

There is not much DVD and video production in the Sámi language. There are some Moomin videos in Sámi; however, they are not available for everyone but schools can borrow them from the learning material bureau. It is inconvenient because the bureau is located in Kautokeino in Norway. In addition, there are some board games and other similar games. Mobile phones do not have comprehensively the Sámi language support because they do not have normally Sámi fonts for text messaging because of producer based electronics capacity and economic questions. Normally it is demanded that telephones are as cheap as possible. Extra language support may demand to cut down other solutions. It is also important to find out in what language the services of other societal sectors, such as stores, banks, post, health care, authorities, and other institutions, are provided. How is the Sámi language brought out in these services? All in all, what kind of linguistic support do these services provide for children? What kind of message about the position of Sámi language do these services give for children? How could the visual and audio stimuli support children's Sámi language proficiency as much as possible? Because of the threatened position of the Sámi language, stimuli that advance all languages should be increased and strengthened. Nowadays, the situation varies from place to place.

A comprehensive language planning is missing. Paying attention to the linguistic matters is important in the context of Sámi schools and this issue is not emphasized in common educational discourse enough. Our development suggestion is that language revitalization programs and strategies should be increased considerably. The processes that already are in progress there give examples on how minorities can improve their linguistic circumstances.

Language Immersion Tepee as a Facilitator of the Sámi Language Learning

Language immersion is a teaching method in which the target language is consciously used in a child's environment, usually at school or a day care center, in the same way as the native language: by hearing it in his or her environment and using it in real-life interactional situations (see Skutnabb-Kangas & Dunbar, 2010). Various subjects can be taught with the target language at school (Creese & Blackledge, 2010; Rodgers, 2006). Teaching through language immersion started in Canada in the 1960s (Genesee, 2012). In New Zealand, the first Kura Kaupapa Māori schools were established in 1985 when the Māori language was in a critical near-death stage. "Kura Kaupapa Māori" refers to Māori-language immersion schools where the philosophy and practice reflect Māori cultural values, with the aim of revitalizing Māori language, knowledge, and culture (Smith, 2005). In Finland, early complete language immersion has been used for teaching the Swedish language since 1987, and it has been studied in the language immersion project at the University of Vaasa (Laurén, 1991), and in Inari Sámi language (Pasanen, 2003).

It is possible to achieve functional bilingualism through language immersion (Cummins, 1998). According to studies, language immersion is an efficient teaching method and does not harm children's development in their native language (Skutnabb-Kangas, 2009). The ability to read is a mechanical skill: after one has learned to read and write, transferring the skill to other languages seems to be easy. Nor do learning difficulties prevent pupils from participating in language immersion (cf. Cummins, 1984).

Language immersion is not completely unproblematic (see e.g. Buss & Mård, 1999), according to findings from Finland, Canada, and Norway (Genesee, 1987; Höglund, 1992). It means that pupils understand the target language as well as native speakers do, but reading and writing do not reach the same level, and, for example, mastery of vocabulary, grammar, and social variation of language remains weaker. On the other hand, better learning outcomes are achieved with language immersion than with any other language teaching method, and it is possible to achieve functional bilingualism through language immersion. In addition, language immersion enhances positive attitudes toward the culture of the target language (Järvinen et al., 1999).

Sámi children lack language support in formal and informal contexts (Hyltenstam et al., 1999; Høier, 2007; Rasmussen & Nolan, 2012; Skutnabb-Kangas & Dunbar, 2010). Research has shown that bilingualism for groups of Sámi pupils has a positive effect on education, but there are also problems. According to Jorun Høier (2007), for example, most bilingual children manage decoding, which means that a child develops an understanding of the function and mechanics of text rather well, but reading comprehension for all children was at least twice as good for the Norwegian language than for Sámi. Tove Skutnabb-Kangas and Robert Dunbar have assessed recommendations for strong models of language instruction in demanding situations. First, it is important to support children's indigenous language for at least the first eight years, to reach high formal level. Second, children's grouping is important. The children should be grouped together by their first language if possible. Third, all children have to become high-level bilinguals. Fourth, all pupils have to be treated in an equal manner in language instruction, and such treatment should be followed up when organizing schooling and education (Skutnabb-Kangas & Dunbar, 2010).

Normally, according to bilingual research literature, the goal of language immersion is bilingualism; in other words, children will learn the target language without harming proficiency in their native language (Christian, 1997; Cummins & Hornberger, 2008). Usually, the term "native language" refers to the language that is spoken at home, while "the target language" is the one that is supposed to be learned through language immersion. The problem with the concepts of "target language" and "native language" when it comes to the status of Sámi is that when the children's native language is lost due to the assimilation process, then it has to become the target language. Thus, we cannot adopt these concepts strictly without focusing on language status first. Indigenous languages are often threatened, so they are at the same time native languages and target languages. The goal with Sámi language immersion should be that the target language becomes the native language (Pasanen, 2003). Therefore, language immersion cannot be designed in isolation from its context, ignoring the prevailing language climate on a societal and individual level. This aspect of language planning should be discussed carefully when implementing a program (see Björklund, 2005).

The Theoretical Model of the Sámi Language Immersion

Various language immersion methods and language nest solutions could enhance the revitalization of the Sámi languages. The language nest solutions offer language and culture immersion for under-school-age children, if the target language is a minority language in danger of extinction. It is based on the idea that a child adopts the target language by hearing it in his or her environment and using it in real-life interactional situations. Based on our findings and previous studies, it seems that several factors constitute successful Sámi language immersion. We have developed a theoretical tepee model (see *Figure 5*) to support both the teaching and learning of Sámi. The form of *lávvu*, a teepee, was chosen because it is a traditional Sámi adobe and resembles a safe place that encloses all actors in the language immersion process. A pupil may learn and improve his or her Sámi proficiency when all factors that affect learning and teaching are considered in the manner illustrated in *Figure 5*. All these factors are also interconnected and form an entity: if some factor does not work, it makes the whole language immersion more difficult to succeed.

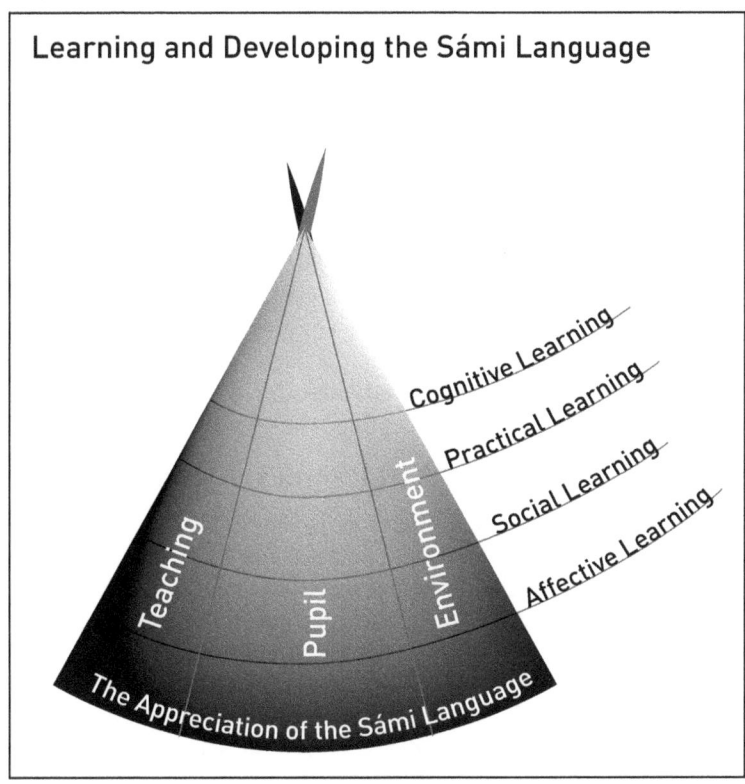

Fig. 5. The Language Immersion Tepee for the Sámi Languages

Appreciation of Sámi lays the foundation for learning language skills and language learning and usage, and for the support for using the language provided by a pupil's home, friends, school, wider environment, and society (see also Giles et al., 1977). Good teaching requires a functional curriculum, cultural-sensitive teaching arrangements, sufficiently motivating and useful learning materials, and teachers' pedagogical and linguistic proficiency. Language learning and teaching are based on indigenous epistemology, in which a holistic view of the school's role is shared, fostering the students' confidence, spirituality, and physical well-being as well as their academic development (see Harrison & Papa, 2005). Pupils' learning is rooted in their talents and starting points as well as in their motivation and language appreciation. Pupil-specific factors can be categorized into four groups: "cognitive factors" refers to the starting point for learning, talents, and learning abilities; "affective factors" means attitudes, values, and motivation; "personality traits" includes self-confidence and self-respect; "social skills" covers communication, interaction, and human relationship skills. These factors form the capacity for learning a language.

When all the above-mentioned factors (pupil, teaching, environment) support Sámi language learning, language immersion may enhance children's Sámi language learning at many levels (cf. Anderson et al., 2001; Harrison & Papa, 2005). Pupils can reach more and more skillful levels of language proficiency.

The illustrations of affective, social, cognitive, and practical learning in *Figure 5* refer to this pattern as well. If learning is described with the verb descriptions of Jerome Bloom's taxonomy, a pupil's progress appears within the four areas of learning through the following keywords or levels in the following way (Bloom, 1956; Chapman, 2005). The goal in language teaching is to reach the higher levels in knowledge, skills, and attitudes that Jerome Bloom (1956) illustrates with the verbs "thinking-doing-feeling" (Krathwohl et al., 1964).

Discussion: A Strong and Vital Sámi Language as the Goal

Language immersion cannot be designed in isolation from its context, ignoring the prevailing language climate at both societal and individual levels. This aspect of language planning should be discussed carefully when implementing a program (see Björklund, 2005) The lávvu-tepee model introduced in this chapter is to be used as a theoretical tool for supporting both the teaching and learning of the Sámi language—or any other target language in language immersion. The model highlights the overall situation of language teaching and the multidimensional nature of the learning and development of Sámi. Therefore, when it comes to the minority languages or indigenous peoples' languages that are in danger of extinction, it is crucial to perceive the whole picture when pursuing a strengthening of the language. Language immersion could be one of the means worth considering: through successful language immersion, children learn to appreciate language skills, use language in various situations, master the language better and better, and become capable of developing the language and advancing its continuity. Language maintenance provides a strong basis for the self-determination of indigenous peoples in global societies.

Making the Dream of a Sámi School Come True: Voices from the Field

The first national Sámi Pedagogy Conference was held in Inari, Finnish Lapland, in 8-9 December 2011. The conference was organized by units that provide Sámi research and education: University of Lapland, Regional State Administrative Agency of Lapland, The Sámi Education Institute and Giellagas Institute. The purpose was to gather Sámi-speaking teachers and educational authorities of the Sámi administrative district and discuss the connection between research and education. The aim was to listen to experts of Sámi education and try to figure out means to support their role and to develop pedagogical methods in Sámi teaching. Giving voice to experts of indigenous peoples' education is important when aiming at promoting development that respects indigenous peoples' values and traditions. We support the idea that the aim of educational research is to support and protect human rights and fundamental freedom and right to pursue social and economic development.

This chapter answers two main questions: what are the most salient disincentives to the realization of Sámi pedagogy in the opinions of the experts of Sámi education and how could the originality of Sámi pedagogy be furthered according to the perceptions of the experts of Sámi education?

Disincentives to the Realization of Sámi Pedagogy

The participants list included disincentives to the realization of Sámi pedagogy and they could be categorized into ten categories.

(1) Economic resources

The learning material office of the Sámi Parliament is responsible for the learning material production in the Sámi language. The state subsidy covers teachers' hiring costs for the municipalities that provide Sámi-speaking teaching and the teaching of Sámi language in the Sámi domicile area. These municipalities get other state subsidies, too, and municipalities are responsible for the practical expenses of education such as acquisitions of teaching materials and other relative costs, such as excursions.

Many participants brought out that Sámi education requires resources and consequently also financial support. Being such a small and special target group, finding finance from the schools' and municipalities' pocket can be difficult. Participants' answers highlighted the need for two kinds of extra-resources: extra-investment to ensure the cultural content so that particular pedagogical practices could be changed at the teaching level and on the other hand, support and

understanding is needed so that teachers could participate in further education. This was expressed, for example, as follows:
> *Municipal authorities do not always understand that Sámi education costs if the aim is to realize Sámi education within its own cultural context.*

Distances are long and means of communication are often difficult. Collaboration with parents and other partners, such as extra resources in teaching personnel, causes extra-costs:
> *Co-operation with parents requires travelling and money.*
> *If we are to exit the classroom, we need a ride, money, and permission.*

Likewise, school heads', rectors', and teachers' actual training can be impeded by the lack of training appropriations. Usually, Sámi teachers' continuing training is free of charge. However, the municipalities normally have to cover teachers' travelling expenses.

(2)   Teachers' loneliness and isolation

Sámi teachers work often alone, far away, and apart. They have an important responsibility to bear. Yet, the support they get at the school level varies. In this research, experts of Sámi education listed various measures of support that are needed: a forum where teachers could share experiences and a system that would support Sámi education in a holistic manner.

Often, communication happens via internet but internet connections do not always work in schools nor can they compensate face-to-face meetings. In addition, teachers do not have time or resources to coordinate these measures of support by themselves but separate actions are needed.
> *Although we do have distance education, the network does not work in a sufficiently flexible way.*

The lack of co-operation occurred at many levels from the school and municipal levels to the state and international levels. The field of Sámi education is relatively scattered, unorganized, and politically unstandardized. A political program for Sámi education is missing. In addition to the Saami Parliamentary Council, Norwegian, Swedish, and Finnish Saami Parliaments have entered developmental needs of Sámi education. However, any actual measures to harmonize educational issues or practical co-operation at the comprehensive school level have not succeeded:
> *It would necessitate a great, revolutionary change in the whole school organization: all the way from the director of education to teachers.*

(3)   Bias and lack of information

To realize Sámi education adequately, a more positive attitude and more information about the special traits of Sámi education are needed. Many of the partic-

ipants highlighted the importance of having a clear definition of Sámi pedagogy because otherwise it is not possible to implement it:
We do not have enough training to know what Sámi pedagogy is.
We should know what we mean by Sámi pedagogy, in other words we need training.
It is not enough that teachers are aware of the concept. The general attitude, support, and understanding are crucial as well. Some participants also expressed their concern about the lack of societal appreciation, prejudices, and even the envy of mainstream population.

It seemed that some people in schools and communities did not understand the meaning of positive discrimination for Sámi education. Resulting from assimilation, the Sámi have lost some of their linguistic and cultural special characteristics including their traditional knowledge system, and that has affected the economic-social well-being of individuals and communities. It takes time to remedy the situation. However, the extra support Sámi education needs is often denied at the municipal decision-making level or at school level by teachers:
Lack of general appreciation of Sámi pedagogy at school.
Due to lack of information, some people may consider Sámi education even a threat. Prejudices may be based on the more general disdain toward multiculturalism and multilingualism:
Lack of pluralism. How to live in a pluralist manner?
Attitudes and strain from the environment: what knowledge/skills are important and appreciated?

(4) Lack of qualified Sámi teachers

The number of Sámi teachers is low and most of them will retire in the near future. Many of the participants were concerned of the availability of qualified Sámi teachers:
Lack of skillful teachers, multiply skilled persons.
Lack of qualified Sámi-speaking teachers.
At the moment, Sámi-speaking teachers are being educated in many institutions. In Finland, there are special quotas for Sámi-speaking teacher students at the Universities of Lapland and Oulu. Norway has provided special Sámi-speaking teacher training already since 1989. Otherwise, it is possible to have the Sámi language as a major in Oulu, Tromsø, Norway, and Umeå, Sweden. Some studies in Sámi language are provided by the University of Helsinki, Finland, as well.

(5) Lack of Sámi pupils

Furthermore, there is lack of Sámi pupils and age groups are small. Often, their school commutes are very long. In addition, it is difficult to reach Sámi children who live in the southern Finland. On the other hand, teaching is not even always available. Therefore, they have not participated in Sámi education sufficiently.

Reaching Sámi children who live outside the Sámi domicile area is problematic because there is no system to remedy the problem.

Most of the Sámi-speaking children do not have Sámi-speaking teaching outside the official Sámi domicile area. The situation is extremely threatening for the continuity of Sámi language. Many generations are lost and proper revitalization measures have not been launched yet systematically and extensively enough.

(6) The chains of the national core curriculum

In Finland, the national core curriculum for comprehensive schools has been appraised even internationally. However, according to the participants in this research, it does not pay attention to the special traits of Sámi culture. Still, all schools are obliged to follow the national core curriculum:

The control: laws and decrees control the Finnish school system that also the Sámi education has to follow.

Finns believe that the Finnish school is the best as is; they think that if you do not study along the Finnish model, you will not succeed.

Sámi teachers are between a rock and a hard place: even if they wanted to teach according to the principles of Sámi pedagogy, they would have to sacrifice the national core curriculum.

Although the curriculum is meant to support and guide teaching, Sámi teachers regarded it as restricting. Likewise, the time for teaching is limited:

There is not enough time to plan teaching alone and together.

Sámi education is often in a contradictory situation: which one is more important—Sáminess or realization of the obligatory curriculum? National curriculum does not solve out problems of Sámi education sufficiently.

(7) Restricting and inflexible practical teaching arrangements

In this research, experts of Sámi education pointed out that teaching practices are based on the traditional Finnish classroom teaching which is usually teacher-led and organized into 45-minute-long lessons.

Time problem: the lesson is 45 minutes, 6 hours a day.
The culture of working alone (1 teacher per classroom).

The Sámi's different conception of time cannot be implemented in the traditional lesson and semester model. Not only teacher colleagues but also pupils find it

difficult to be flexible. Sámi model would have student- and task-oriented way of organizing lessons and breaks and semesters.
> *Too deep-rooted models control the school system too much.*

The Finnishnized school—too much classroom teaching when we should design teaching together with all classes, in themes.

(8) Lack of learning materials

There is not enough learning material in the Sámi language or it is old and not culturally relevant.
> *Lack of learning materials in schools in all three [Sámi] languages.*

Often, Sámi teachers prepare learning materials by themselves but they do not have enough time for all this. Similarly, there are no teachers' manuals in the Sámi language except for a few school subjects. Moreover, the problem in translated materials is their weak cultural basis. All in all, there is not enough material to support teaching, not enough producers of learning materials, or work force to adjust the existing materials to Sámi pedagogy:
> *Lack of ancillary staff.*
> *Overall, the school provides little information about the Sámi.*

(9) Lack of the Sámi language proficiency

Language is the foundation of teaching and culture. If there are no Sámi speakers, the whole Sámi pedagogy is shaken. There is lack of qualified Sámi-speaking subject teachers. Pupils' language proficiency varies greatly and parents do not necessarily speak the Sámi language at home or with other relatives. Sámi families' language policy can be partly undefined because of the history of assimilation. According to the act of education, only part of education is provided in the Sámi language and that is too little.
> *There is no Sámi School in Finland (although there should be). There is just the Finnish School.*

(10) The Sámi's insecurity

Many of the participants recognized their own responsibility as promoters of Sámi education but were insecure. And yet, without the Sámi people selves being active and setting the example, Sámi education cannot strengthen:
> *The feeling that I cannot realize it (what if I hurt the children in case I cannot act in the right way).*
> *You could trust in your own Sáminess and want out Finnishness that affects everything, even your thoughts. You should dare to be Sámi at your work place as well.*

Moreover, teachers' activity is not enough but parents and children have to participate. Without their participation, teachers have too many responsibilities to bear:

> *Parents do not participate in school activities.*

Means of Strengthening Sámi Pedagogy

The participants were asked to discuss how to strengthen Sámi education. Their practical experiences, thoughts, and ideas were categorized into four partly overlapping groups.

(1) Positive attitudes and resources

Positive attitudes toward Sámi pedagogy were considered a salient factor in the realization of Sámi education. According to group discussions, Sámi pedagogy should become appreciated by the school community and also wider in the society.

> *The school administration should commit to Sámi pedagogy so that Sámi teachers were not left alone when implementing teaching.*

The participants of this study highlighted that the arousal of positive attitudes necessitates knowledge of Sámi pedagogy. Schools should provide in-service and continuing education in Sáminess and its educational special traits. Sámi teachers are true multiple skilled people who should also be recruited as prospective teachers' in-service educators and learning material producers more than before.

Certain practical means could promote positive attitudes, too. Sáminess could be brought out in a positive manner in theme days at school and for example, the Sámi national day could be celebrated to consciously highlight Sámi culture in an appreciative way. However, in order to avoid having Sáminess as just a single topic once a year, it should become a cross-curricular theme.

(2) A Sámi curriculum and the Sámi language

It was considered essential to create and implement a Sámi curriculum where the Sámi language has a central role. The curriculum cannot just be an application of the Finnish curriculum but it should be based on the Sámi's premises.

The core principle of curriculum design should be equality and parity. Sámi children should have the same rights to have education that is based on their own culture than other children have—and equality should not be used against Sámi children:

> *As the dominant language at school is Finnish, Sámi children remain a minority.*
>
> *We need a totally separate and own Sámi School.*

The quality schooling provides also information about all local cultures to every pupil. That is why Sámi contents should be presented to everybody.

(3) Cultural-sensitive teaching arrangements

According to the data, Sámi teachers among other experts of Sámi education wanted to wreck stereotype conceptions or prejudices concerning Sámi children's background or future.

Not all Sámi people are fishermen or reindeer herders.

Traditional livelihoods are plied also as compound livelihoods, for example together with tourism and other service industry. The proportion of natural livelihoods in revenue and workforce is not very large but the cultural meaning is significant. They are not just livelihoods or professions but parts of a unique life style. Some of the Sámi still earn their living in traditional livelihoods but a considerable proportion of the Sámi work in modern professions (The Saami Parliament, 2008). Still, the old myths seem to hinder the development also in the Sámi's own cultural context. The Sámi conception of time, place, and knowledge necessitates a breakaway from the Finnish teaching practices. Even the smallest details make a good example:

The classroom curtains could illustrate Sámi craftsmanship and colors.

The school decoration could exploit traditional handicrafts. The Sámi construction culture and seasons were previously tied to their nomadic living style and hunting culture. It can also be taken into account in teaching arrangements:

Pupils should be able to spend time in a tepee by the fire, do things that are part of Sámi culture and learn new.

All this should happen through a holistic educational idea rather than offering just singular parts of Sámi culture. The Sámi group is small and therefore, new practices should be developed to make teaching more integrated and stable. It would be important to try new approaches—a sort of pedagogical revolution:

Why could you not teach math and handicraft simultaneously?

Here we talk about how to implement traditional knowledge in the everyday practices of school.

(4) The ideal Sámi School

The participants described their idea of an ideal Sámi School where everyone would speak the Sámi language and their language proficiency would be furthered through constant usage:

There would be learning materials and various stages and levels to enhance language proficiency.

This school would be everyone's school and "not a lonely island". The school would support Sámi families and strengthen the family-centeredness which is typical of the Sámi culture. Thus, the school would support the Sámi's storytelling tradition that would transmit traditions from one generation to another:

> *There would be a day care center and a retirement home with the school premises.*

Likewise, the principles of peer learning, joint learning and action could be reinforced:

> *Older pupils could guide the younger ones—and learn something new themselves.*

Togetherness, trust, appreciation, and responsibility for various school tasks would enhance pupils' positive self-image and be based on the Sámi storytelling tradition. Consequently, school premises and physical environment would be molded to represent the Sámi culture. The connection with nature should be preserved and thus, nature education and "night schools" would support the understanding of nature—the nature has offered the setting for life and livelihoods.

> *What would be the physical environment—there would not be a school building but an eternal camping school.*

Everyone should share the knowledge and understanding about the objectives and goals of school and education and all this would result in the well-being of Sámi culture and Sámi children:

> *...so that the child would do well and have a strong self-esteem.*

The Developmental Drum of Sámi education

The conference participants' answers showed that the core of the Sámi School is to secure the Sámi language and the Sámi language teaching. In addition, it is important to strengthen the special characteristics of the Sámi culture and the contents of the Sámi pedagogy that are drawn from the culture. Instead of providing singular pieces of the Sámi culture, the Sámi School is an entity and its values and operation are based on the Sámi values and way of thinking and the needs of the Sámi community and the multicultural society.

These research results correspond to the recent publications that have brought out epistemological questions about research on indigenous peoples as well as special questions about rearing and education. Studies on indigenous peoples' teaching and education around the world seem to elicit information that concerns our research as well (see Balto, 2008; Darnell & Hoëm, 1996; Hirvonen, 2004/2003; Lipka et al., 1998).

Based on the perceptions from the field, we designed a model, a Sámi education developmental drum (see *Figure 6*) adopted from the Sámi culture. This drum symbolizes a thought that it is about the time to develop Sámi pedagogy, to use the drum for the Sámi-speaking Sámi education. All Finnish Sámi drums represent a three-dimensional worldview: upper, middle, and lower worlds. First they had transcendental meanings but later on more practical ones. Here, the drum also has three worlds. The Sámi language is located in the middle as it is considered the most important factor. Other significant features represent teaching and other practical issues taking place at school while the third dimension covers societal environment and conditions.

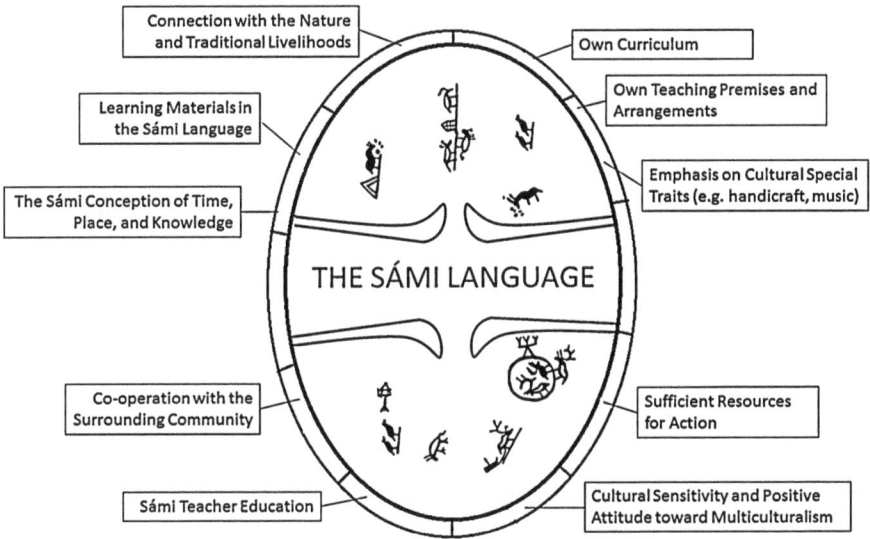

Fig. 6. The developmental drum of Sámi education

Language is one of the most significant factors of identity and its importance cannot be undermined when discussing the future of the Sámi as an indigenous people. Thus, it is placed in the center of the model, in the middle world. In Finland, pupils who speak the Sámi language are taught mainly in the Sámi language at the Sámi district. This wording may lead to a decrease in the Sámi language teaching among the decreasing number of Sámi pupils. In order to avoid the extinction of the Sámi language, strengthen its development and avoid language change and assimilation trends, teaching in one's native language should be guaranteed at every school level unequivocally. Furthermore, it is important to promote positive attitudes toward indigenous peoples among other populations. At the Sámi School, the Sámi language would be the teaching language of every school subject. Naturally, it is the question of economic investments, too:

the organization of Sámi education should be financially supported even when provided outside the Sámi domicile area.

The sustenance and development of language nest and language immersion methods are crucial when aiming at strengthening the Sámi language. They are important but need to be accompanied with language revitalization. Sámi language courses should be arranged as in-service training so that employees' ability to speak and write in the Sámi language would improve and they would appreciate the Sámi language. The Sámi language could become a more active working language.

The school level, the upper world in the drum, includes special school-level arrangements. In order to not lose out to the Finnish language and the Finnish curriculum and school system, the Sámi School needs a curriculum, teaching premises and arrangements, and Sámi learning materials of its own cultural premises. The Sámi selves have to be active and highlight the necessity of strengthening their own culture within school practices. The connection with the nature, the coexistence of the human being with the nature and traditional livelihoods is important. It means that reindeer pasturage, fishing waters, courses, small-scale agriculture, picking culture and handicrafts are considered a part of cultural knowledge. The question is about appreciating cultural capital in schools (see Yosso, 2006).

Pupils should be provided with positive experiences related to their own culture through play, story-telling, action, and participation. Teaching should be adjusted with the yearly cycle of the local Sámi community, traditional seasonal work and changes that take place in the nature (Rasmus, 2004). If pupils cannot participate in reindeer herding and seasonal activities related to it (e.g. reindeer roundup) or if they are not allowed to see items that represent the Sámi culture, handicrafts, art, or other objects, at school, they will not see their cultural heritage appreciated by the system, and in the end, that may harm their sense of humanity (see also Chacón et al., 2010).

The central task of the school is to support the Sámi pupils' identity: the school must provide chances to the development of a healthy self-esteem so that the Sámi pupils can have their Sámi identity without assimilation in the mainstream population. To sum, it is necessary to take action to rationalize teacher education (cf. Cuban, 1993), strengthen virtual education, and create language revitalization programs. Consequently, the third world in the drum represents the overall conditions that make the Sámi education possible.

Sufficient economic resources are needed to start the action. Sámi-speaking teacher education should pay special attention to the teaching methods suitable for teaching pupils with various linguistic backgrounds, to the forms of highlighting the Sámi culture, and to the problems of minority cultures. This kind of extra training should be arranged in the Sámi domicile area when it would be possible to participate in the training alongside work without high expenses (cf. Näkkäläjärvi & Rahko, 2007). Natural providers of education would be the Sámi University College (Kautokeino, Norway), Sámi Education Institute (Inari, Finland), University of Lapland (Rovaniemi, Finland), and Giellagas Institute at the University of Oulu (Oulu, Finland)—in collaboration. Likewise, early childhood education needs Sámi-speaking early childhood educators and preschool teachers. Because most of the Sámi children live outside the Sámi domicile area, it would be important to develop virtual education and provide necessary personnel and material resources to implement it. The Sámi Education Institute has already started this work.

The starting point of Sámi education is challenging compared to the mainstream culture because it does not have all the material and support that are normally provided for language teaching. Sámi parliaments have, however, listed available learning materials to let educators and other interested know about these materials. Actually the worldview differs from the mainstream culture insomuch that knowledge about learning should be constructed from a new point of view. Teachers' in-service training could seize on this situation. Teachers should be informed of indigenous educational practices.

In addition, the results suggest that co-operation with the wider Nordic community is valuable both to Sámi teachers and pupils. Teaching should support pupils' identify with their national cultural heritage and their sense of solidarity with the Sámi people who live in different countries. Respect for the Sámi culture means also respect for multiculturalism. Indeed, Sámi education could get new stimuli from the cultural sensitive education in North-America and New Zealand where students' culture and experienced are given emphasis (e.g. Kirkeness, 1992, 2003; Lipka et al., 1998; Macfarlane, 2004). For example, the community elders take part in education as the bearers and transmitters of culture (Stiegelbauer, 1996).

Discussion

It was not until the 1970s when the Sámi education took root in school and the Sámi's own opinions were taken into account in educational planning since the missionary period. Still, many things should change to make the Sámi School reform happen along the ideas of experts of Sámi education. Is this kind of a change possible?

There are many theorists whose ideas encourage us to interfere in today's educational practices, shake inequality and dissolve ideas of normative knowledge, meanings, and subjects. Let us mention Gilles Deleuze and Félix Guattari's (1987) concepts of the assemblage, becoming, and rhizomatics.

Michel Foucault's (e.g. 1982) writings about resistances, practices of the self, and parrhesia/fearless speech and Judith Butler's (1997) thoughts about performative politics, discursive agency, and collectivities. At times, these concepts seem arcane but their purpose is to introduce ways of interfering or question the prevailing "normality" of the school. Besides, Deleuze and Guattari (1987) noted that they do not even want to become understood but actually misunderstood!

Education is one of the most powerful state structures that instill and renew the dominant ideology. Education and rearing have conscious and unconscious influence on us. Education does not teach just practical skills, such as reading and math, but embeds societal moral rules, norms, and culture that teach how to speak and think right (see Hier, 2003). Consequently, it is possible to look for optional phrasings of question and challenge normative interpretations and ideologies. Indeed, unspoken viewpoints in the field of education and rearing belong to this category as well. If become informed of these issues, we are aware and realize what kinds of appreciations, practices, models, hidden effects, resources, and social relationships are included in the daily schooling. At its best, awareness leads to critical discussions and enables us see new perspectives.

In order to develop the Sámi School, it is necessary to listen to the active realizers of Sámi education, namely Sámi teachers. Not only do they have plenty of tacit knowledge but also "conscious silence" that we have to listen to and take into account when aiming at strengthening Sámi pedagogy. At the Sámi teachers' ideal school, premises are open, accessible and welcome to everyone; a place where everyone listens, hears, discusses; where teachers have time and interest in pupils' ideas, thoughts, experiences, feelings, fantasies, and hopes; where mutual trust between various generations and genders is present; where the conception of knowledge and knowing has new forms; and where experiential and communal learning are given space (cf. Youdell, 2011). The ideal school is the one where cultural sensitivity and policies are recognized and acknowledged and which strengthens the cultural identity of its members.

The Sámi culture has already seen glimpses of this kind of a school and therefore educational researchers and developers should not give up on looking for a better education. We want to provide starting points for a discussion that would hopefully lead to the more positive utilization of aspects of Sámi culture in the education system in Finland, and perhaps, it would contribute to the similar discussion in the whole indigenous world. The dream of a Sámi School and Sámi pedagogy is realistic.

Sámi Pedagogy

The indigenous people's right to develop education based on their own premises must be at the center when planning new reforms. Fixing some individual educational issues is not enough when aiming to strengthen Sámi pedagogy but solutions to the wider entities have to be figured out piece by piece. As the Sámi community does not yet have wider educational self-government, ideas of becoming independent are needed. Embedding Sámi pedagogy also challenges the reconstruction of teacher education.

The indigenous education is tied to the Western concepts of progress and to the globalism. Indigenous peoples have their own forms of local knowledge, practical expertise, and culturally specific means of transmitting knowledge (Crystal, 2000). Our book is to support cultural continuity and the survival of indigenous peoples. In addition to a secure land base, this survival means freedom of religious, cultural, and linguistic expression, rights which members of dominant national groups all too often take for granted. Indigenous peoples' participation in education is an essential part of transforming abstract policy formulations into long-awaited results that make a real difference in peoples' lives. Indigenous education is characterized by emancipatory ideologies of indigenous sovereignty, self-determination, and cultural revalorization. We want to point out the potential of an indigenous pedagogy based on context-specific learning systems to promote cultural and language revitalization.

There is a constant need for an analysis of the relationships between the dominant culture and indigenous populations. This analysis helps us to understand not only the specific cases mentioned in this selection but also general problems arising when different cultures meet. Many indigenous peoples now are becoming increasingly confident in their assertion of the validity of their own knowledge and wisdom (Teasdale, 1995, p. 589).

The need for developing Sámi education is evident. Balto (1997) names family connections, concrete experiences, the nature and environment as the key words of Sámi education (see also Balto, 2008). This action resembles reform pedagogy where collaboration, conceptualization, learner activity, and constructivism are central concepts (Bruner, 1963; Dewey, 1997/1938; Illeris, 1974; Montessori, 1964/1916; Vygotsky, 1976; Øzerk, 1999, 2006). Therefore, creating a pedagogy that would match local educational situations seems the most necessary and topical. Jan Henry Keskitalo (1999) refers to integrating communality which means a principle of seeing Sámi education as a part of the multicultural local community and whose position and situation are solved according to the principles of inclusive education (see also Høgmo, 1989).

When talking about Sámi pedagogy, it is important to define some core concepts: Sámi pedagogy, Sámi education, and Sámi school are ambiguous concepts. The concept of Sámi school is already in use in Norway and Sweden. In Norway, it refers to the school system in the administrative district of the Sámi language where the Sámi curriculum is applied in schools. The Sámi school is meant for all pupils who live in that district. In practice, the Sámi school operates in a pluralist multilingual context, and therefore, the Sámi school and education refer to Sámi-speaking, Norwegian-speaking, and bilingual education. School-specific language-political definitions of policy have been made locally (Keskitalo, 2010). In Sweden, the Sámi School is governed by the Sámi school administration, *Sameskolstyrelsen*. The Sámi School in Sweden covers grades 1–6 (Sameskolstyrelsen, 2013).

Sámi education means education that focuses on Sámi-speaking teaching of the Sámi language and culture. It is worth distinguishing Sámi-speaking teaching from the teaching of the Sámi language. The first refers teaching that takes place in the Sámi language while the latter means teaching of the school subject of Sámi language. The subject can be either the subject of the first language or the second language depending on situation.

Sámi pedagogy means the Sámi's own pedagogy that acknowledges the historical-cultural phenomena or burden related to the Sámi's position and strengthens the special features of the Sámi culture through teaching and classroom arrangements. The special features of Sámi pedagogy are intertwined with the paradigmatic changes of teaching that aim at squaring the learning environment and the learner's role with the Sámi culture (Keskitalo & Määttä, 2011). Sámi pedagogy is therefore connected to the science of education: it combines the basic principles of the science of education with the traditional Sámi education. When introducing Sámi pedagogy in academic use, we can talk about Sámi school knowledge (J. H. Keskitalo, 2009).

Sámi pedagogy combines the Sámi and western education so that teaching arrangements include as little as possible components of traditional western school culture. For example, the Finnish school was founded on Herbart-Zillerism which is an educational trend emphasizing teachers' authority position. This German educational philosophy still is evident although the new school has taken root in Finnish education, too (Paksuniemi, 2009). However, the Sámi pedagogy aims at pulling down the colonized practices of school which means that awareness of the indigenous people's needs and possibilities is a salient part of the change of school.

International research has brought out the core differences and problems between western and indigenous pedagogies (Kanstrup-Jensen, 2006; de Plevitz, 2007). Ninetta Santoro et al. (2011) highlight that teachers who work with indigenous pupils must understand the pupils' conception of knowledge, worldview, and conception of a human being. Therefore, experiential learning in informal situations and in collaboration with parents and the elders of the local indigenous community should be emphasized in teaching. Moreover, teachers should become aware of how pupils' backgrounds affect their learning outcomes. Teachers networking is seen a means of helping teachers with these aspects of their work (Legare et al., 1998; Santoro et al., 2011). A study conducted in Canada reported that teachers named the lack of collegial cooperation as one of the negative sides of their work. At the same time, numerous demands and expectations are faced at teachers. Opportunities of sharing experiences and having guidance at work would be important means of supporting teachers' work (Wimmer et al., 2009).

Many questions still remain unstudied and we look forward to continue our work in this important area. Political and educational fields need direct and continuous courage to enhance indigenous peoples' education. Moreover, it requires hard work and perseverance. Indeed, according to Barbara Seidl and Gloria Friend (2002), "the development of sophisticated, culturally relevant pedagogies is a process that requires commitment over time and lived experience" (p. 427).

We need to invest in the children and their teachers—the human capital. Tania M. Li (2000) has pointed out that the future of indigenous peoples "does not lie in state handouts" (p. 24). The education revolution begins and ends with people: teaching them, giving them skills and the confidence to do their very best for themselves and their communities. This pursuit means that people have to loyal to their own needs and have to find the most suitable ways of self-fulfillment but simultaneously noticing other people and their needs (Uusiautti & Määttä, 2012, p. 268). We want to emphasize the human willingness and ability to change and strive for acceptance and respect for cultural diversity.

References

Adair, G. (1984). The Hawthorne effect: a reconsideration of the methodological artifact. *Journal of Applied Psychology, 69*, 334–345.

Ahonen, A. (2008). Kouluissa ei viihdytä, mutta miksi. Pohjoissuomalaisten oppilaiden kouluviihtyvyyttä selittävien tekijöiden tarkastelua [People do not enjoy themselves at schools, but why. Research on school satisfaction in Northern Finland]. In M. Lairio, H. L. T. Heikkinen, and M. Penttilä (Eds.), *Koulutuksen kulttuurit ja hyvinvoinnin politiikat [Education cultures and politics of well-being]* (pp. 195-211). Helsinki: Finnish Educational Research Association.

Aikio, A. (2003). Sámi skuvla – máŋggakultuvrralaš servodaga skuvla. In V. Hirvonen (Ed.), *Sámi áddejupmi ja sámi skuvla [Sámi understanding and Sámi education]* (pp. 66–70). Nordic Sami Educational Research Conference Kautokeino in November 7th–9th 2001. SUC Report 1-(2003). Guovdageaidnu: Sámi allaskuvla/Samisk høgskole.

Alderson, P. (2001). Research by children: rights and methods. *International Journal of Social Research Methodology: Theory and Practice, 4*(2), 139-153.

Alderson, P., & Morrow, V. (2011). *The ethics of research with children and young people: a practical handbook*. London: Sage.

Althusser, L. (1970). *Ideology and ideological state apparatuses*. La Pensée. Retrieved from Lenin and Philosophy and Other Essays, Monthly Review Press 1971. http://www.marxists.org/reference/archive/althusser/1970/ideology.htm

Anaya, J. (2011). *Report of the Special Rapporteur on the situation of human rights and fundamental freedoms of indigenous people*. United Nations. Retrieved from http://unsr.jamesanaya.org/country-reports/the-situation-of-the-sami-people-in-the-sapmi region-of-norway-sweden-and-finland-2011

Anderson, L. W., & Burns, R. B. (1989). *Research classrooms. The study of teachers, teaching, and instruction*. Oxford: Pergamon Press.

Anderson, L. W., Krathwohl, D. R., Airasian, P. W., Cruikshank, K. A., Mayer, P. R. Pintrich, J. R., & Wittrock, M. C. (Eds.). (2001). *A taxonomy for learning, teaching & assessing: a revision of Bloom's taxonomy of educational objectives*. New York, NY: Addison Wesley Longman.

Anzaldúa, G. (1987/1999). *Borderlands – La frontera*. San Francisco: Aunt Lute Books.

Aro, M. (2009). Effect of orthography on reading acquisition: theoretical and practical implications. In J. J. Ijäs & N. Ø. Helander (Eds.), *Sáhkavuoruin sáhkan. Sámegiela ja sámi girjjálašvuođa muhtin áigeguovdilis dutkanfáttát* (pp 9-21). (Dieđut 1). Guovdageaidnu: Sámi allaskuvla.

Artzt, A. F., & Armour-Thomas, E. (2002). *Becoming a reflective mathematics teacher: a guide for observations and self assessment*. Mahwah: Lawrence Erlbaum Associates.

Atkinson, P. (1992). *Understanding ethnographic texts. Qualitative research methods 25*. Newbury Park: Sage.

Atkinson, P., & Hammersley, M. (1994). Ethnography and participant observation. In N. Denzin & Y. Lincoln (Eds.), *Handbook of qualitative research* (pp. 248-261). Thousand Oaks, CA: Sage.

Bailey, F., Burkett, B., & Freeman, D. (2008). The mediating role of language in teaching and learning: a classroom perspective. In B. Spolsky & F. M. Hult (Eds.), *The handbook of educational linguistics* (pp. 606-625). Malden: Blackwell.

Bakmand, B. (2000). National language planning – why (not)? *Intercultural Communication*, 3. Retrieved from http://www.immi.se/intercultural/nr3/bakmand.htm

Ball, J. (2012). *Enacting indigenous research ethics through community-university partnerships*. University of Victoria. Retrieved from http://www.ecdip.org/ethics/

Balto, A. (1997). *Sámi mánáidbajásgeassin nuppástuvvá [Sámi childrearing in change]*. Oslo: ad Notam Gyldendal.

Balto, A. (2008). *Sámi oahpaheaddjit sirdet árbevirolaš kultuvrra boahttevaš buolvvaide: dekoloniserema akšuvdnadutkamuš Ruota beale Sámis [Sámi teachers transforming traditional culture to the next generations: action research about decolonization in Sápmi of Sweden]*. Guovdageaidnu: Sámi allaskuvla.

Barfield, T. (Eds.) (1997). *The dictionary of anthropology*. Oxford: Blackwell.

Barker, J., & Waller, S. (2003). "Never work with children": the geography of methodological issues in research with children. *Qualitative Research, 3*(2), 207-227.

Barnhardt, R. (2002). Domestication of the ivory tower: institutional adaptation to cultural distance. *Anthropology & Education Quarterly, 33*(2), 238-249.

Barnhardt, R., & Kawagley, A. O. (2005). Indigenous knowledge systems and Alaska native ways of knowing. *Anthropology and Education Quarterly, 36*(1), 8-23.

Barron, A. (2002). Traditional knowledge, indigenous culture and intellectual property rights. In *Samisk forskning og forskningsetikk [Sámi research and research ethics]* (pp. 56-87). (Publications No. 2.) Oslo: Forskningsetiske komiteer.

Beresford, B. (1997). *Personal accounts: involving disabled children in research*. York: University of York Social Policy Research Unit.

Bergland, E. (2001). *Samisk skole og samfunn: plattform for pedagogisk utviklingsarbeid [Sámi School and society: platform for educational improvement]*. Dieðut – research report no. 4. Guovdageaidnu: Sámi Instituhtta.

Bishop, R., & Glynn, T. (1999). *Culture counts. Changing power relations in education*. Palmerston North: Dunmore Press.

Björklund, S. (2005). Toward trilingual education in Vaasa/Vasa, Finland. *International Journal of the Sociology of Language, 171*(1), 23-40.

Bloom, B. S. (1956). *Bloom's taxonomy*. Retrieved from http://www.nwlink.com/~donclark/hrd/bloom.html

Boekaerts, M. (1995). The interface between intelligence and personality as determinants of classroom learning. In D. H. Saklofske & M. Zeidner (Eds.), *International handbook of personality and intelligence* (pp. 161-183). New York, NY: Plenum Press.

Bourdieu, P. (1977). *Outline of a theory of practice.* Cambridge: Cambridge University Press.
Bourdieu, P., & Passeron, J. C. (1990). *Reproduction in education, society and culture.* London: Sage.
Brewer, J., & Hunter, A. (1990). *Multimethod research. A synthesis of styles.* Thousand Oaks, CA: Sage.
Brown, L., & Strega, S. (Eds.) (2005). *Research as resistance: critical, indigenous, & anti-oppressive approaches.* Toronto: Canadian Scholars' Press.
Bruner, J. S. (1963). *The process of education.* New York, NY: Vintage.
Bull, T. (2002). Kunnskapspolitikk, forskningsetikk og det samiske samfunnet [Knowledge politics, research ethics and the Sámi society]. In Den nasjonale forskningsetiske komité for samfunnsvitenskap og humaniora [The National Research Ethical Committee for Social Sciences and Humanities] (Ed.), *Samisk forskning og forskningsetikk [Sámi research and research ethics]* (pp. 6-21). Oslo: Forskningsetiske komiteer.
Buss, M., & Mård, C. (1999). *Ruotsin ja suomen kielen kielikylvyn kartoitus Suomen peruskouluissa lukuvuonna 1998/99 [Survey on the Swedish and Finnish language immersion in Finnish comprehensive school in semester 1998-1999].* Vaasa: University of Vaasa. Retrieved from: http://www.uwasa.fi/materiaali/pdf/isbn_951-683-811-1.pdf
Butler, J. (1997). *Excitable speech: a politics of the performative.* London: Routledge.
Capdeville, S. (2009). Suomen saamenkielisten painotuotteiden alkutaival: Ensimmäisistä saamennoksista saamenkieliseen kirjallisuuteen [The beginning of the Finland's Sámi language publications: from the first Sámi translations to Sámi literature]. In K. Ruppel (Ed.), *Omin sanoin [In your own words].* Helsinki: Kotimaisten kielten tutkimuskeskus. Retrieved from http://scripta.kotus.fi/www/verkkojulkaisut/julk6/Omin_ sanoin.pdf
Carpelan, C., Kulonen, U.-M., Pulkkinen, R., Seurujärvi-Kari, I., Porsanger, J., Korhonen, O., Svonni, M., & Beck, L. D. (Eds.) (2004). *The encyclopaedia of Saami culture.* Helsinki: University of Helsinki. Retrieved from http://www.helsinki.fi/~sugl_smi/senc/en/johdanto.htm
Castro, N. T. (2007). Doing ethnographic research among indigenous peoples. Diliman: University of the Philippines.
Chacón, H., Yanez, F., & Larriva, G. (2010). Ecuadorian Amazonian cultures: theoretical approaches to the training of researchers. In J. C. Llorente, K. Kantasalmi, & S. J. de Dios (Eds.), *Approaching indigenous knowledge. Complexities of the research process* (pp. 47–68). Helsinki: University of Helsinki.
Chapman, A. (2005). *Bloom's and others original concepts.* Retrieved from: http://www.businessballs.com/bloomstaxonomyoflearningdomains.htm
Christian, D. (1997). *Profiles in two-way immersion education.* McHenry, IL: Delta Systems.

Clark, A. (2005). Listening to and involving young children: a review of research and practice. *Early Child Development and Care, 175*(6), 489-505.

Coffey, A. (1999). *The ethnographic self: fieldwork and the representation of identity.* London: Sage.

Collins, J. (2009). Social reproduction in classrooms and schools. *Annual Review of Anthropology, 38*, 33-48.

The Constitution of Finland (731/1999). Finlex. Retrieved from Finlex data based http://www.finlex.fi/fi/laki/ajantasa/1999/19990731

The Constitution of the Russian Federation. (1993). Retrieved from http://www.constitution.ru/en/10003000-01.htm

Creese, A., & Blackledge, A. (2010). Translanguaging in the bilingual classroom: a pedagogy for learning and teaching? *The Modern Language Journal, 94*(1), 103-115.

Creswell, J. W. (2003). *Research design: qualitative, quantitative, and mixed methods approaches.* Thousand Oaks, CA: Sage.

Crystal, D. (2000). *Language death.* Cambridge: Cambridge University Press.

Cuban, L. (1993/1984). *How teachers taught. Constancy and change in American classrooms 1880–1990.* (2nd ed.) New York, NY: Teachers College Press.

Cummins, J. (1984). *Bilingualism and special education: issues in assessment and pedagogy.* Clevedon: Multilingual Matters.

Cummins, J. (1998). Immersion education for the millennium: What have we learned from 30 years of research on second language immersion? In M. R. Childs & R. M. Bostwick (Eds.), *Learning through two languages: research and practice. Second Katoh Gakuen International Symposium on Immersion and Bilingual Education* (pp. 34-47). Japan: Katoh Gakuen.

Cummins, J., & Hornberger, N. H. (2008). *Bilingual education.* New York, NY: Springer.

Darnell, F., & Hoëm, A. (1996). *Taken to extremes: education in the far North.* Oslo: Scandinavian University Press.

Dehyle, D., & Swisher, K. (1997). Research in American Indian and Alaska native education: from assimilation to self-determination. In M. Apple (Ed.), *Review of research in education* (pp. 113-194). Washington, DC: AERA.

Deleuze, G., & Guattari, F. (1987). *A thousand plateaus.* Minneapolis, MN: University of Minnesota Press.

Denzin, N., & Lincoln, Y. (2000). Introduction: the discipline and practice of qualitative research. In K. Denzin, & Y. Lincoln (Eds.), *Handbook of qualitative research* (pp. 1-28). Thousand Oaks, CA: Sage.

de Plevitz, L. (2007). Systematic racism: the hidden barrier to educational success for Indigenous school students. *Australian Journal of Education, 51*(1), 54-71.

Dewey, J. (1997/1938). *Experience and education.* New York, NY: Touchstone.

Díaz de Rada, A. (2007). School bureaucracy, ethnography and culture: conceptual obstacles to doing ethnography in schools. *Social Anthropology, 15*(2), 205-222.

Dockett, S., Einarsdottir, J., & Perry, B. (2009). Research with children: ethical tensions. *Journal of Early Childhood Research, 7*(3), 283-298.

Eddy, E. M. (1997). Theory, research, and application in educational anthropology. In G. D. Spindler (Ed.), *Education and cultural process. Anthropological approaches* (pp. 4-25). (3rd ed.). Prospect Heights, IL: Waveland Pres.

Eidheim, H. (2007). Terapiatapahtuman havainnoinnista, kulttuurisesta ja ammatillisesta kompetenssista [About the observation of therapy event, cultural and professional competence]. In H. Eidheim & V. Stordal (Eds.), *Kulttuuritietoisia kohtaamisia. Sosiaali- ja terapiatyöstä saamelaisalueella [Culture-conscious encounters. About social and therapy work in the Sámi district]* (pp. 53-69). Rovaniemi: Pohjois-Suomen sosiaalialan osaamiskeskus.

Engin, M. (2011). Research diary: a tool for scaffolding. *International Journal of Qualitative Methods, 10*(3), 296-306.

Ellsworth, E. (1997). *Teaching positions: difference, pedagogy and the power of address*. New York, NY: Teachers College, Columbia University.

Erickson, F., & Gutierrez, K. (2002). Comment: culture, rigor, and science in educational research. *Educational Researcher, 31*(8), 21-24.

Eriksen, K. (2007). *Iešmearrideapmi hástá suverenitehta. Ságastallan álgoálbmogiid iešmearrideamis Ovttastuvvan Našuvnnaid álgoálbmotjulggaštus –bargojoavkkus [Self-determination challenges sovereignty. A discussion about indigenous peopls' self-determination in the Indigenous Peoples Declation work group of United Nations]*. (Master's thesis). Rovaniemi: University of Lapland.

Evans, R. (2001). *The human side of school change: reform, resistance, and the real-life problems of innovation*. San Francisco, CA: Jossey-Bass.

Fargas-Malet, M., McSherry, D., Larkin, E., & Robinson, C. (2010). Research with children: methodological issues and innovative techniques. *Journal of Early Childhood Research, 8*(2), 175-192.

Fitzpatrick, K. (2011). Stop playing up! Physical education, racialization and resistance. *Ethnography, 12*(2), 174-197.

Flewitt, R. (2005). Conducting research with young children: some ethical issues. *Early Childhood Development and Care, 175*(6), 553-565.

Fontana, A., & Frey, J. H. (2005). The interview. From neutral stance to political involvement. In N. K. Denzin & Y. S. Lincoln (Eds.), *The handbook of qualitative research* (pp. 695-728). London: Sage.

Ford, R. (1997). Educational anthropology. Early history and educationist contributions. In G. D. Spindler (Ed.), *Education and cultural process. Anthropological approaches* (pp. 26-45). (3rd ed.) Prospect Heights, IL: Waveland Press.

Ford, K., Sankey, J., & Crisp, J. (2007). Development of children's assent documents using a child-centred approach. *Journal of Child Health Care, 11*(1), 19-28.

Forsey, M. G. (2010). Ethnography as participant listening. *Ethnography, 11*(4), 558-572.

Foucault, M. (1982). The subject and power. In H. L. Dreyfus & P. Rabinow (Eds.), *Michel Foucault: Beyond hermeneutics and structuralism* (pp. 208-226). Brighton: Harvester.
Freire, P. (2006/1970). *Pedagogy of the oppressed.* New York, NY: Continuum.
Geertz, C. (1973). *The interpretation of cultures.* New York, NY: Basic Books.
Geertz, C. (2010). *Life among the anthros.* Princeton: Princeton University Press.
Genesee, F. (1987). *Learning through two languages: studies of immersion and bilingual education.* Cambridge, MA: Newbury House Publishers.
Genesee, F. (2012). *The suitability of French immersion for students who are at risk: a review of research evidence.* McGill University. Retrieved from http://www.psych.mcgill.ca/perpg/facgenesee/Suitability%20of%20Immersion%20for%20AtRisk%20Students.pdf
Giles, H., Bourhis, R. Y., & Taylor, D. M. (1977). Towards a theory of language in ethnic group relations. In H. Giles (Ed.), *Language, ethnicity, and intergroup relations* (pp. 307-348). New York, NY: Academic Press.
Goetz, J. P., & LeCompte, M. D. (1984). *Ethnography and qualitative design in educational research.* London: Academic Press.
Gonagaslaš girko-, oahpahus- ja dutkandepartemeanta [The royal church, education and research ministry]. (1997). *10-jagi vuođđoskuvlla sámi oahppoplánat (O97S) [10-year Primary School Curriculum].* Oslo.
Goode, D. A. (1986). Kids, culture and innocents. *Human Studies, 9,* 83-106.
Goodlad, J. I., Klein, F. M., & Tye, K. A. (1979). The domains of curriculum and their study. In T. H. Quinn & M. Hennelly (Eds.), *Curriculum inquiry: the study of curriculum practice* (pp. 43-76). New York, NY: McGraw-Hill.
Gordon, T., Holland, J., & Lahelma, E. (2001). Ethnographic research in educational settings. In P. Atkinson, A. Coffey, S. Delamont, J. Lofland, & L. Lofland (Eds.), *Handbook of ethnography* (pp. 188-203). London: Sage.
Gordon, T., & Lahelma, E. (2004). Etnografinen katse koulutuspolitiikkaan [Ethnographic look at educational policy]. *Kasvatus, 35*(1), 66–78.
Gothóni, R. (1997). Eläytyminen ja etääntyminen kenttätutkimuksessa [Empathy and distancing the field study]. In A. Viljanen & M. Lahti (Eds.), *Kaukaa haettua. Kirjoituksia antropologisesta kenttätyöstä [Far-fetched. The writings of an anthropological field work* (pp. 136-148). Helsinki: Suomen Antropologinen Seura.
Graue, E. M., & Walsh, D. J. (1998). *Studying children in context: Theories, methods and ethics.* Thousand Oaks, CA: Sage.
Grover, S. (2004). Why won't they listen to us? On giving power and voice to children participating in social research. *Childhood, 11*(1), 81-93.
Grunnloven, § 110 a. Grunnlovsbestemmelse 27. mai 1988 nr. 432. Retrieved from http://www.lovdata.no/all/hl-18140517-000.html
Gundem, B. B. (1990). *Læreplanpraksis og læreplanteori: en introduksjon til læreplanområdet [Curriculum in practice and curriculum theory: an introduction to curriculum field].* Oslo: Universitetsforlaget.

Gupta, A., & Ferguson, J. (1996). Discipline and practice: "The Field" as site, method, and location in anthropology. In A. Gupta & J. Ferguson (Eds.), *Anthropological locations, boundaries and grounds of a field science* (pp. 1-46). Berkeley, CA: University of California Press.

Halinen, P. (2011). Arkeologia ja saamentutkimus [Archeology and Sámi research]. In I. Seurujärvi-Kari, P. Halinen, & R. Pulkkinen (Eds.), *Saamentutkimus tänään [Sámi research today]* (pp. 130-176). Helsinki: Finnish Literature Association.

Hall, S. (2003). Kulttuuri, paikka, identiteetti [Culture, place, identity]. In O. Löytty & M. Lehtonen (Eds.), *Erilaisuus [Dissimilarity]* (pp. 85-128). Tampere: Vastapaino.

Hammersmith, J. A. (2007). *Converging indigenous and western knowledge systems: implications for tertiary education.* (PhD thesis). University of South Africa.

Hannerz, U. (2003). Kulttuurin määritelmien yhteentörmäys [Collision with culture definitions]. In M. Lehtonen & O. Löytty (Eds.), *Erilaisuus [Dissimilarity]* (pp. 213-232). Tampere: Vastapaino.

Harrison, N. (2005). The learning is in-between: the search for a metalanguage in indigenous education. *Educational Philosophy and Theory, 37*(6), 871-884.

Harrison, B., & Papa, R. (2005). The development of an indigenous knowledge program in a New Zealand Maori-Language Immersion School. *Anthropology & Education Quarterly, 36*(1), 57-72.

Heikkilä, M. (2002). Eettisiä ongelmia yhteiskuntatieteellisessä tutkimuksessa [Ethical problems in social science research]. In S. Karjalainen, V. Launis, R. Pelkonen, & J. Pietarinen (Eds.), *Tutkijan eettiset valinnat [Researcher's ethical choices]* (pp. 165-176). Tampere: Gaudeamus.

Heikkilä, M., & Sahlström, F. (2003). Om användning av videoinspelning i fältarbete [About the use of videoing in field work]. *Pedagogisk Forskning i Sverige, 8*(1-2), 24–41.

Helander, E., & Kailo, K. (1999). *Ei alkua ei loppua. Saamelaisten puheenvuoro [No begin no end. Sámi people speak up].* Helsinki: LIKE.

Henriksen, J. B., Scheinin, M., & Åhrén, M. (2005). *Pohjoismaisen saamelaissopimuksen taustamateriaalia. Pohjoismainen saamelaissopimus: 13. marraskuuta 2002 nimitetyn suomalais-norjalais-ruotsalais-saamelaisen asiantuntijatyöryhmän 27. lokakuuta 2005 luovuttama luonnos [Background Material of the Nordic Sámi Convention. Nordic Sámi Convention: An outline handed in 27 Oct 2005 by a Finnish-Norwegian-Swedish-Sámi work group established in 13 Nov 2002]* (pp. 263-314). Oslo: Arbeids- og inkluderingsdepartementet.

Henson, R. K., Hull, D. M., & Williams, C. S. (2010). Methodology in our education research culture: toward a stronger collective quantitative proficiency. *Educational Researcher, 39*(3), 229-240.

Hermes, M. (2000). The scientific method, Nintendo, and Eagle feathers: rethinking the meaning of "culture-based" curriculum at an Ojibwe tribal school. *Qualitative Studies in Journal of Studies in Education, 13*(4), 387–400.

Hertting, K., & Alerby, E. (2009). Learning without boundaries: to voice indigenous children's experiences of learning places. *The International Journal of Learning, 16*(6), 633-647.

Hier, S. P. (2003). Probing the surveillant assemblage: on the dialects of surveillance practices as processes of social control. *Surveillance and Society 1*(3), 399-411.

Hiim, H., & Hippe, E. (1998). *Læring gjennom opplevelse, forståelse og handling. En studiebok i didaktikk [Learning through experience, understanding and handling. A study book of didactics]*. Universitetsforlaget, Oslo.

Hill, M. (1997). Participatory research with children. Research review. *Child and Family Social Work, 2*, 171-183.

Hill, R., & May, S. (2013). Non-indigenous researchers in indigenous language education: ethical implications. *International Journal of the Sociology of Language, 219*, 47-65.

Hirvonen, V. (2004/2003). *Sámi culture and the school: reflections by Sámi teachers and the realization of the Sámi School*. Karasjok: ČálliidLágádus.

Hirvonen, V., & Balto, A. (2008). Iešmearrideapmi sámi oahppo- ja skuvlensuorggis [Self-governance in Sámi educational field]. In J. B. Henriksen (Ed.), *Sámi Iešmearrideapmi [Sámi self-governance]. Gáldu čála. Álgoálbmotvuoigatvuodaid áigečála*, 2/2008, 104–123.

Hoëm, A. (1978). *Sosialisering: en teoretisk og empirisk modellutvikling [Socialisation: an theoretical and empiric model elaboration]*. Oslo: Universitetsforlaget.

Hoëm, A. (1995). Sámemánáid ovddešáiggi bajássaddandilli [Sámi children and education in the past]. In R. Erke & A. Høgmo (Eds.), *Identitehta ja eallin. Artihkalčoakkáldat moanaálbmotlaš servodagain, mas sápmelaččaid dilli lea guovddážis [Identity and life—Sámi culture in a multicultural society]* (pp. 40-55). (2nd ed.) Guovdageaidnu: Sámioahpahusráđđi.

Hollins, E. R. (2008). Foreword. In H. Kohl (Ed.), *Culture in school learning: revealing the deep meaning* (pp. xi-xii). New York, NY: Routledge.

Hoppers, C. A. O. (2002). Indigenous knowledge and the integrations of knowledge systems. Towards a conceptual and methodological framework. In C. A. O. Hoppers (Ed.), *Indigenous knowledge and the integration of knowledge systems: towards a philosophy of articulation* (pp. 2–22). Claremont: New Africa Books.

hooks, b. (1994). *Teaching to transgress: education as the practice of freedom*. New York, NY: Routledge.

Hostetler, K. (2005). What is "good" education research? *Educational Researcher, 34*(6), 16-21.

Huttunen, L., Löytty, O., & Rastas, A. (2005). Suomalainen monikulttuurisuus. Paikallisia ja ylirajaisia suhteita [Finnish multiculturalism: local and transitional relations]. In A. Rastas, L. Huttunen, & O. Löytty (Eds.), *Suomalainen vieraskirja. Kuinka käsitellä monikulttuurisuutta? [Finnish guest book. How to handle multiculturalism?]* (pp. 16–40). Tampere: Vastapaino.

Hyltenstam, K., Stroud, C., & Svonni, M. (1999). Språkbyte, språkbevarande, revitalisering. Samiskans ställning i svenska Sápmi. In K. Hyltenstam (Ed.), *Sveriges sju inhemska språk – ett minoritetsspråksperspektiv [The seven national languages of Sweden – The minority perspective]* (pp. 41-97). Lund: Studentlitteratur.

Høgmo, A. (1989). *Norske idealer og samisk virkelighet: om skoleutvikling i det samiske området [Norwegian idealism and the Sámi reality: school improvement in the Saami areas]*. Oslo: Gyldendal.

Høier, J. (2007). *Lese for å lære. Tospråklige utfordringer i utvikling av lesekom-petanse i et minoritetsperspektiv [Reading in order to learn. Bilingual expectations in progress of reading skills in minority perspective]*. Tromsø: Eureka forlag.

Höglund, H. (1992). *Läsförståelse i svenska och finska hos språkbadselever [Reading comprehension of language-immersion pupils in Swedish and Finnish]*. Vaasa: University of Vaasa.

Illeris, K. (1974). *Problemorientering og deltagerstyring: oplæg til en alternativ didaktik [Problem orientation and participant management: proposal for an alternative education]*. København: Munksgaard.

ILO. (1989). *C169 - Indigenous and Tribal Peoples Convention, (No. 169)*. Genève: International Labour Organization.

Irwin, K. (1992). Towards theories of Maori feminisms. In R. du Plessis (Ed.), *Feminist voices: women's studies texts for Aotearoa/New Zealand* (pp. 1-21). Auckland: Oxford University Press.

James, A. (2001). Ethnography in the study of children and childhood. In P. Atkinson et al. (Eds.), *Handbook of ethnography* (pp. 246-257). London: Sage.

James, A., Jenks, C., & Prout, A. (1998). *Theorizing childhood*. Cambridge: Polity Press.

Johnson, R. B., & Onwuegbuzie, A. J. (2004). Mixed methods research: a research paradigm whose time has come. *Educational Researcher, 33*(7), 14-26.

Josefsen, E. (2010). *The Saami and the national parliaments: Channels for political influence*. Geneva/New York, NY: IPU and UNDP.

Judén-Tupakka, S. (2000). *Daya naisten maailman välittäjänä: kehitysyhteistyöprojektiin osallistuneita yläegyptiläisiä kyläkätilöitä koskeva tutkimus [Daya as a mediating structure of the life of women: research about midwifes at the development cooperation project in highland in Egypt]*. Helsinki: University of Helsinki.

Judén-Tupakka, S. (2003). Kasvatusantropologia – tutkimuskohteena siirtymärituaalit, enkulturaatio ja kulttuuritransitio [Educational anthropology – transitional rituals, enculturation, and cultural transition as a research target]. In H. Sinevaara-Niskanen, & R. Rajala (Eds.), *Kasvatuksen yhteisöt – uupumista, häirintää vai yhteisöllistä kasvua? [Educational communities – fatigue, disturbance, or communal development?]* (pp. 311-323). Rovaniemi: University of Lapland.

Järvinen, H.-M., Nikula, T., & Marsh, D. (1999). Vieraskielinen opetus [Instruction in foreign-language]. In K. Sajavaara, & A. Piirainen-Marsh (Eds.), *Kielenoppimisen kysy-*

myksiä [Queries about language learning] (pp. 229–258). Jyväskylä: University of Jyväskylä.

Kanstrup-Jensen, A. (2006). *Indigenous education and knowlegde – a de-legitimised concept in the education for all strategies.* DIR - Research Center on Development and International Relations Department of History, International and Social Studies, Aalborg University Development Research Series, Working Paper No. 136.

Keskitalo, J. H. (2009). Sámi máhttu ja sámi skuvlamáhttu: teorehtalaš geahčastat [Sámi knowledge and Sámi school knowledge: theoretical overview]. *Sámi dieđalaš áigečála, 1–2*, 62–75.

Keskitalo, P. (2010). *Saamelaiskoulun kulttuurisensitiivisyyttä etsimässä kasvatusantropologian keinoin [Cultural sensitivity in the Sámi school through educational anthropology].* (PhD thesis., Dieđut 1/2010.) Guovdageaidnu: Sámi allaskuvla.

Keskitalo, P., & Määttä, K. (2011). *Sami pedagogihka iešvuođat /Saamelaispedagogiikan perusteet / The Basics of Sami Pedagogy / Grunderna i samisk pedagogik / Основы саамской педк.* Rovaniemi: Lapland University Press.

King, L., & Schiermann, S. (2004). *The challenge of indigenous education: practice and perspectives.* Paris: Unesco.

Kinos, J. (2002). Kohti lapsilähtöisen varhaiskasvatuksen teoriaa [Toward child-centered early childhood education theory]. *Kasvatus, 33*(2), 119–132.

Kirkeness, V. J. (1992). *First nations and schools: triumphs and struggles.* Toronto: Canadian Education Association.

Kirkeness, V. J. (2003). Aboriginal Education in Canada: a retrospective and a prospective. In V. Hirvonen (Ed.), *Sámi áddejupmi ja sámi skuvla. Davviriikkalaš sámi skuvladutkiid konferánsa Guovdageainnus 7.–9.11.2001 [Sami understanding and Sami education. Nordic Sami Educational Research Conference Kautokeino November 7th–9th 2001]* (pp. 51–65). Guovdageaidnu: Sámi allaskuvla.

Kjærnsli, M., Lie, S., Olsen, R. V., & Roe, A. (2007). *Tid for tunge løft. Norske elevers kompetanse i naturfag, lesing og matematikk i PISA 2006 [Time for knowledge lift. Norwegian pupils' knowledge in nature subject, reading and mathematics in PISA 2006].* Oslo: Universitetsforlaget.

Kneller, G. F. (1966). *Educational anthropology: an introduction.* New York, NY: John Wiley.

Kohonen, V., & Leppilampi, A. (1992). Kohti yhteistoiminnallista koulukulttuuria – koulunjohdollinen koulutus uusien haasteiden edessä [Towards cooperational school culture – school administration education facing the new challenges]. In K. Hämäläinen & A. Mikkola (Eds.), *Koulun kehittämisen kansainvälisiä virtauksia [International trends in developing the school]* (pp. 31-56). Helsinki: VAPK-publication.

Krathwohl, D. R., Bloom, B. S., & Masia, B. B. (1964). *Taxonomy of educational objectives: the classification of educational goals. Handbook II: Affective Domain.* New York, NY: David Mckay.

Krokfors, L., Suominen, L., Wäre-von Hedenberg, M., & Uusitalo. (2008). *Uudet kirjaimet ja numerot. Käsinkirjoittaminen ja kirjoittamaan opetus [New letters and numbers. Handwriting and writing instruction]*. Helsinki: Finnish National Board of Education.

Kroskrity, P. V., & Field, M. C. (Eds.) (2009). *Native American language ideologies: beliefs, practices, and struggles in Indian country*. Tuscon, AZ: University of Arizona Press.

Kuokkanen, R. (2000). Towards an "Indigenous Paradigm" from a Sami perspective. *The Canadian Journal of Native Studies, 20*(2), 411–436.

Kuokkanen, R. (2007). *Reshaping the university: responsibility, indigenous epistemes, and the logic of the gift*. Vancouver: UBC Press.

Kvernmo, S. E., & Stordal, V. (1991). Fra same til akademiker — fra deltaker til observatør? Erfaringer fra utviklingen av en samisk helsetjeneste [From the Sámi to academics — from participant to observer? Experiences of enhancing the Sámi health care]. In M. Aikio & K. Korpijaakko (Eds.), *Samesymposium [Sámi symposium]* (pp. 71–85). Rovaniemi: University of Lapland.

Kylli, R. (2005). *Kirkko saamelaisten maalla – yhteentörmäyksiä vai yhteisymmärrystä? [The church in the Sámi area – clashes or consensus?]* (PhD thesis.) Oulu: University of Oulu.

Labaree, D. F. (2003). The peculiar problems of preparing educational researchers. *Educational Researcher, 32*(4), 13-22.

Lag 2009: 724. Lag om nationella minoriteter och minoritetsspråk. Retrieved from http://www.notisum.se/rnp/sls/lag/20090724.htm

Lauhamaa, P., Rasmus, E.-L., & Judén-Tupakka, S. (2006). Saamelaiskasvatus sosialisaation, enkulturaation ja identiteetin käsitteiden valossa [The Saami education through concepts of socialisation, enculturation and identity]. In T. Martikainen (Ed.), *Ylirajainen etnisyys: monikulttuurinen Suomi 2000-luvulla [Over-boundary ethnicity: multicultural Finland in the 21st century]* (pp. 190–211). Helsinki: Finnish Literature Society.

Laurén, C. (Ed.) (1991). *Kielikylpymenetelmä: Kielen käyttö mielekkääksi [Language immersion: Toward meaningful language usage]*. Vaasa: University of Vaasa.

Lavallée, L. F. (2009). Practical application of an indigenous research framework and two qualitative indigenous research methods: sharing circles and Anishnaabe symbol-based reflection. *International Journal of Qualitative Methods 8*(1), 21-40.

Legare, L., Pete-Willett, S., Ward, A., Wason-Ellam, L. & Jessen Williamson, K. (1998). *Diverting the mainstream: aboriginal teachers reflect on their experiences in the Saskatchewan provincial school system*. Final report. Retrieved from http://www.education.gov.sk.ca/diverting-mainstream.

Lehtonen, M. (2004/1996). *Merkitysten maailma [The world of the meanings]*. (5th ed.) Tampere: Vastapaino.

Lerkkanen, M.-K. (2003). *Learning to read: reciprocal processes and individual pathways*. Jyväskylä: University of Jyväskylä.

Li, T. M. (2000). *Articulating indigenous identity in Indonesia: Resource politics and the tribal slot.* Berkeley, CA: University of California.

Lillemyr, O. F., Søbstad, F., Marderb, K., & Flowerday, T. (2010). Indigenous and non-Indigenous primary school students' attitudes on play, humour, learning and self-concept: a comparative perspective. *European Early Childhood Education Research Journal, 18*(2), 243–267.

Lincoln, Y. S., & Guba, E. G. (1985). *Naturalistic inquiry.* Thousand Oaks, CA: Sage.

Lipka, J., Mohatt, G. V., & the Ciulistet Group. (Eds.) (1998). *Transforming the culture of schools. Yup'ik Eskimo examples.* Mahwah: Lawrence Erlbaum Associates.

Lipka, J., & Yanez, E. (1998). Identifying and Understanding Cultural Differences: Toward a Culturally based Pedagogy. In J. Lipka, G. V.Mohatt, & the Ciulistet Group (Eds.), *Transforming the culture of schools. Yup'ik Eskimo Examples* (pp. 111-137). Mahwah: Lawrence Erlbaum Associates.

Loether, C. (2009). Language revitalization and the manipulation of language ideologies. In P. V. Kroskrity & M. C. Field (Eds.), *Native American language ideologies: beliefs, practices, and struggles in Indian country* (pp. 238-254). Tuscon, AZ: University of Arizona Press.

London, N. A. (2002). Curriculum convergence: an ethno-historical investigation into schooling in Trinidad and Tobago. *Comparative Education, 38*(1), 53–72.

Lowe, L. (2005/2003). Heterogeneity, hybridity, multiplicity: marking Asian-American differences. In J. Evans & A. Braziel (Eds.), *Theorizing diaspora* (pp. 132-155). Malden: Blackwell.

Lyster, R. (1999). Classroom-oriented research in immersion. In C. Laurén (ed.), *En modell för språk I daghem och skola: språkbadsdidaktik i Canada, Katalonien och Finland [A model for language at kindergarten and school: language immersion in Canada, Catalonia and Finland]* (pp. 81–92). University of Vaasa, Vaasa.

Länsman, A.-S. (2008). Kenelle saamentutkija tutkii? [Whom does a Sámi researcher do research for?] In K. Lempiäinen, O. Löytty, & M. Kinnunen (Eds.), *Tutkijan kirja [The researcher's manual]* (pp. 87-98). Tampere: Vastapaino.

Macfarlane, A. H. (2004). *Kia hiwa ra! Listen to culture – Maori students' plea to educators.* Wellington: New Zealand Council for Educational Research.

Magga, O. H., & Skutnabb-Kangas, T. (2001). The Saami languages: the present and the future. Endangered languages, endangered lives 25.2.2001. *Cultural Survival Quarterly, 25*(2), 26-31, 51.

Mandell, N. (1991). The least adult role in studying children. In F. C. Waksler (Ed.), *Studying the social worlds of children: sociological readings* (pp. 38-59). London: Falmer Press.

Máhttodepartemeanta, Sámediggi, & Oahpahusdirektoráhtta. (2007). *Máhttolokten. Sámi oahppoplánabuvttus [Knowledge Raising. Sámi curriculum].* Oslo: Oahpahusdirektoráhtta. Retrieved from http://www.sametinget.no/kunde/filer/Kunnskapsloftet %20samisk_NORDSAMISK(1).pdf

Malinowski, B. (1984). *Argonauts of the Western Pacific: an account of native enterprise and adventure in the Archipelagos of Melanesian New Guinea.* Prospect Heights, IL: Waveland Press.

Manninen, L., Hallia, O., Hautala, T. K., Kumpulainen, M., Latvala, J., Laukkanen, M., Mäkinen, M., Nurmi, I., Rovio, T., & Sääskilahti, N. (Eds.) (1994). *Jargon: kulttuuriantropologian englanti–suomi-oppisanasto [Jargon: Cultural anthropological English-Finnish dictionary].* Jyväskylä: Jyväskylä University Students' Union.

Marker, M. (2000). Lummi identity and white racism: when location is a real place. *Qualitative Studies in Education, 13*(4), 401–414.

Mayall, B. (2000). The sociology of childhood in relation to children's rights. *The International Journal of Children's Rights, 8*, 243-259.

Metsämuuronen, J. (2006). Laadullisen tutkimuksen perusteet [The basics of qualitative research]. In J. Metsämuuronen (Ed.), *Laadullisen tutkimuksen käsikirja [Handbook of qualitative research]* (pp. 79-144). Helsinki: International Methelp.

Mills, G. E. (2007). *Action research. A guide for the teacher researcher.* Upper Saddle River, NJ: Merrill/Prentice Hall.

Mohanty, C. T. (1994). On race and voice: challenges for liberal education in the 1990s. In H. A. Giroux & P. McLaren (Eds.), *Between borders: pedagogy and the politics of cultural studies* (pp. 146-166). New York, NY: Routledge.

Montessori, M. (1964/1916). *The Montessori method.* New York, NY: Schocken Books.

Morrow, V., & Richards, M. (1996). The ethics of social research with children: an overview. *Children and Society, 10*, 28-40.

Moss, P., & Petrie, P. (2002). *From children's services to children's spaces.* London: Routledge Falmer.

Murillo, L. A. (2009). "This great emptiness we are feeling": toward a decolonization of schooling in Simunurwa, Colombia. *Anthropology & Education Quarterly, 40*(4), 421-437.

Myrvoll, M. (2002). Knocking on heaven's door. In *Samisk forskning og forskningsetikk: den nasjonaleforskningsetiske komité for samfunnsvitenskap og humaniora [Sámi research and research ethics: the national committee of social sciences and humanities] (NESH)* (pp. 45–55). Oslo: De nasjonale forskningsetiske komitéer.

Myrvoll, M. (2005). *Samisk begynneropplæring: evaluering [Sámi language instruction at first grades: evaluation].* Tromsø: Høgskolen i Tromsø.

Nelson-Barber, S., & Dull, V. (1998). Don't act like a teacher! Images of effective instruction in a Yup'ik Eskimo classroom. In J. Lipka, G. V. Mohatt, & The Ciulistet Group (Eds.), *Transforming the culture of schools: Yup'ik Eskimo Examples* (pp. 91-105). Mahwah: Lawrence Erlbaum Associates.

Newbury, D. (2001). Diaries and Fieldnotes in the Research Process. *Research Issues in Art Design and Media*, 1, 1-17.

Nind, M. (2011). Participatory data analysis: a step too far? *Qualitative Research, 11*(4), 349-363.

Nurmi, K. E., & Kontiainen, S. (1995). A framework for adult learning in cultural context: mediating cultural encounters. In A. Kauppi, S. Kontiainen, K. E. Nurmi, J. Tuomisto, & T. Vaherva (Eds.), *Adult learning in a cultural context* (pp. 65–71). Helsinki: University of Helsinki, Lahti Research and Training Centre.

Nystad, I. M. K. (2003). *Mannen mellom myte og modernitet [The man between myth and modernity]*. Nesbru: Vett & Viten.

Näkkäläjärvi, E., & Rahko, R. (2007). Saamen kielen ja saamenkielisen opetuksen asema ja merkitys [The position and meaning of the Sámi language and Sámi-speaking teaching]. In S. Pöyhönen, & M.-R. Luukka (Eds.), *Kohti tulevaisuuden kielikoulutusta. Kielikoulutuspoliittisen projektin loppuraportti [Toward the future language education. The final report of the project of language educational policy]* (pp. 253-274). Jyväskylä: University of Jyväskylä.

Ogbu, J. U. (1988). Black education: a cultural-ecological perspective. In H. P. McAdoo (Ed.), *Black families* (pp. 169-184). Thousand Oaks, CA: Sage.

Ogbu, J. U. (1992). Understanding cultural diversity and learning. *Educational Researcher, 21*(8), 5-24.

Opas, M. (2004). Mitä on uskontoetnografia [What is religion ethnography]? In O. Fingerroos, M. Opas, & T. Taira (Eds.), *Uskonnon paikka [The place for religion]* (pp. 153-182). Helsinki: Finnish Literature Society.

Oser, F., Dick, A., & Paltry, J. (1992). *Effective and responsible teaching*. San Franciso, CA: Jossey-Bass.

Oskal, N. (2008). The question of methodology in indigenous research. A philosophical exposition. In H. Minde, S. Jentoft, H. Gaski, & G. Midré (Eds.), *Indigenous peoples: self-determination, knowledge, indigeneity* (pp. 331-345). Eburon: Delft.

Osterman, K. F., & Kottkamp, R. B. (1993). *Reflective practice for educators: improving schooling through professional development*. Newbury: Corwin Press.

Paksuniemi, M. (2009). *Alakansakoulunopettajaseminaarin opettajakuva lukuvuosina 1921-1945 rajautuen oppilasvalintoihin, oppikirjoihin ja oheistoimintaan [The teacher image in the lower primary school teachers' college of Tornio in 1921-1945]*. (Acta Universitatis Lapponiensis No. 161.) Rovaniemi: University of Lapland.

Pasanen, A. (2003). *Kielipesä ja revitalisaatio: Karjalaisten ja inarinsaamelaisten kielipesätoiminta [A language nest and revitalization: Language nest activity among the Karelian and the Inari Sámi]*. Helsinki: University of Helsinki.

Patton, M. Q. (1990). *Qualitative evaluation and research methods*. Thousand Oaks, CA: Sage.

Peltokorpi, E.-L., Määttä, K., & Uusiautti, S. (2012). How to ensure ethicality of action research in the classroom. *World Journal of Education, 2*(3), 32-42.
Piaget, J. (1978/1977). *The development of thought: equilibration of cognitive thought.* Oxford: Basil Blackwell.
Pollock, M. (1997). Class discussion: comparing Hutterite education and an inner city school. In G. D. Spindler (Ed.), *Education and cultural process: Anthropological approaches* (pp. 548-557). Prospect Heights, IL: Waveland.
Porsanger, J. (2007). *Bassejoga čáhci: gáldut nuortasámiid oskkoldaga birra álgoálbmotmetodologiijaid olis [The Water of the Sacred River: The Sources of the Indigenous 251 Working with Traditional Knowledge: Communities, Institutions, Information Systems, Law and Ethics. Religion of the Eastern Sami Examined Within the Framework of Indigenous Methodologies].* Kárášjohka: Davvi Girji.
Porsanger, J. (2011). The Problematisation of the Dichotomy of Modernity and Tradition in Indigenous and Sami contexts. In. J. Porsanger, & G. Guttorm (Eds.), *Working with Traditional Knowledge: Communities, Institutions, Information Systems, Law and Ethics. Writings from the Arbediehtu Pilot Project on Documentation and Protection of Sami Traditional Knowledge* (pp. 225-252). Guovdageaidnu: Sámi allaskuvla.
Porsanger, J., & Guttorm, G. (Eds.) (2011). *Working with Traditional Knowledge: Communities, Institutions, Information Systems, Law and Ethics. Writings from the Arbediehtu Pilot Project on Documentation and Protection of Sami Traditional Knowledge.* Guovdageaidnu: Sámi allaskuvla.
Powell, M. B. (2000). P.R.I.D.E.: the essential elements of a forensic interview with an Aboriginal person. *Australian Psychologist, 35,* 186-192.
Powell, M., & Smith, A. (2009). Children's participation rights in research. *Childhood, 16*(1), 124-142.
Prior, D. (2007). Decolonising research: a shift toward reconciliation. *Nursing Inquiry, 14*(2), 162–168.
Programa de educación intercultural multilingüe de Centroamerica. (2008a). Qchwinqil twitz xjan tx'otx'. Tqaqin kol. Dirección general de educación bilingüe intercultural. Digebi. Guetamala: Colección Nuestra vida.
Programa de educación intercultural multilingüe de Centroamerica. (2008b). Qak'aslem pa. Abya yala. Ro' qana'oj qetamab'al. Dirección general de educación bilingüe intercultural. Digebi. Guetamala: Colección Nuestra vida.
Punch, S. (2002). Research with children: the same or different from research with adults? *Childhood, 9*(3), 321-341.
Päivänsalo, P. (1953). *Lappalaisten lastenhoito- ja kasvatustavoista [About the Childcare and Upbringing of Lapps].* Helsinki: Suomen kasvatus-sosiologinen yhdistys.
Pääkkönen, M. (1990). *Grafeemit ja konteksti: tilastotietoja suomen yleiskielen kirjaimistosta [The graphemes and context: statistics of Finnish standard language alphabet].* Helsinki: SKS.

Rantala, T. (2005). *Oppimisen iloa etsimässä: kokemuksen etnografiaa alkuopetuksessa* [*Looking for the joy of learning: early experience in teaching ethnography*]. (Acta Universitatis Lapponiensis No. 88.) Rovaniemi: University of Lapland.

Rantala, T. (2007). Kokemuksen etnografia – avain koulun arjen tunteisiin [Experience of ethnography - the key everyday emotions at school]. In E. Syrjäläinen, A. Eronen, & V.-M. Värri (Eds.), *Avauksia laadullisen tutkimuksen analyysiin [Views about qualitative research analysis]* (pp. 126-158). Tampere: Tampere University Press.

Rasmus, E. L. (2004). *Saamelaisen identiteetin merkitys Utsjoen nuorille. Kasvatusantropologinen tutkimus saamelaisten maailmankuvasta ja identiteetistä [The Sámi Identity and Its Meaning for the Sámi Youth in Utsjoki. Educational Anthropological Research about Worldview and Identity of the Sámi People]*. Rovaniemi: University of Lapland.

Rasmussen, T., & Nolan, J. S. (2012). Reclaiming Sámi languages: indigenous language emancipation from East to West. *International Journal of the Sociology of Language, 209*, 35–55.

Regalsky, P., & Laurie, N. (2007). 'The school, whose place is this'? The deep structures of the hidden curriculum in indigenous education in Bolivia. *Comparative Education, 43*(2), 231-251.

Rodgers, D. M. (2006). Developing content and form: Encouraging evidence from Italian content-based instruction. *The Modern Language Journal, 90*(3), 373-386.

Rønning, W. (2002). *Likeverdig skole i praksis. Presentasjon av ei kartlegging [Equal education in practice. Presentation of a survey]*. Bodø: Nordlandsforskning.

The Saami Parliament (2008). *The Sámi in Finland*. Inari: The Sámi Parliament.

Sámiráđđi. (1989). *Saamelaispoliittinen ohjelma* [Sámi political program]. Ohcejohka.

Saaranen-Kauppinen, A., & Puusniekka, A. (2006). Triangulaatio [Triangulation]. In *KvaliMOTV - Menetelmäopetuksen tietovaranto [KvaliMOTV - The method of teaching knowledge pool]*. Tampere: Database of social sciences.

Sahlström, F. (2008a). *Från lärare till elever, från undervisning till lärande: utvecklingslinjer i svensk, nordisk och internationell klassrumsforskning [From teacher to student, from teaching to learning: trends in Swedish, Nordic and international classroom research]*. Stockholm: Vetenskapsrådet.

Sahlström, F. (2008b). Där och då, här och nu : några reflektioner över möjligheterna för samtalsanalytisk lärandeforsking att analysera lärande mellan situationer [There and then, here and now: some reflections on the possibilities for conversation analytic learning scattered to analyze learning situations between]. In M. Enell-Nilsson, & T. Männikkö (Eds.), *Erikoiskielet, käännösteoria ja monikielisyys: Vakki-symposium XXVIII Vaasa 8. - 9.2.2008* [Special Languages, Translation Theory and Multilingualism: Vakki Symposium XXVIII. Vasa 8 – 9 Feb 2008] (pp. 10-30). Vasa: VasaPublication.

Said, E. W. (1978). *Orientalism*. New York, NY: Pantheon Books.

Saikkonen, T.-L., & Miettinen, S. (2005). Kouluetnografi – missä olet? Tutkijaposition paikantamista koulukontekstissa [School ethnographer - where are you? Locating the researcher position at the school context]. *Kasvatus, 36*(4), 307-319.

Salo, U.-M. (1999). *Ylös tiedon ja taidon ylämäkeä. Tutkielma koulun maailmoista ja järjestyksistä [Top of knowledge and skill hill. Thesis about worlds of school and order]*. (Acta Universitatis Lapponiensis, No. 24.) Rovaniemi: University of Lapland.

Sameskolstyrelsen. (2013). Jokkmokk. Retrieved from http://www.sameskolstyrelsen.se/

Santoro, N., Reid, J.-A., Crawford, L., & Simpson, L. (2011). Teaching indigenous children: listening to and learning from indigenous teachers. *Australian Journal of Teacher Education, 36*(10), 64-76.

Sara, J. I. (1987). *Skuvla – lagasbiras Sámi birrasiin [School - immediate vicinity of the Sámi environments]*. Oslo: Det Norske Samlaget.

Sara, M. N. (2003). Árbevirolaš sámi dieđut ja máhtut sámi vuođđoskuvllas [Traditional Sámi knowledge and skills at Sámi Primary School]. In V. Hirvonen (Ed.), *Sámi skuvla plánain ja praktihkas. Mo dustet O97S hástalusaid? Reforbma 97 evalueren [Sámi school in plan and practice]* (pp.121-138). Kárášjohka: ČalliidLágádus.

Sarason, S. B. (1971). *The culture of the school and the problem of change*. Boston: MA: Allyn and Bacon.

Sarivaara, E. (2012). *Statuksettomat saamelaiset. Paikantumisia saamelaisuuden rajoilla [Non-status Sámi. Locations within Sámi borderlands]*. (PhD thesis, University of Lapland, Finland.) Kautokeino: Sámi University College.

Schanche, A. (2002). Saami skulls, anthropological race research and the repatriation question in Norway. In C. Fforde, J. Hubert, & P. Turnbull (Eds.), *The dead and their possessions: repatriation in principle, policy and practice* (pp. 47-58). London: Routledge.

Schoorman, D., & Bogotch, I. (2010). What is a critical multicultural researcher? A self-reflective study of the role of the researcher. *Education, Citizenship and Social Justice, 5*(3), 249-264.

Seidl, B., & Friend, G. (2002). Leaving authority at the door: equal-status community-based experiences and the preparation of teachers for diverse classrooms. *Teaching and Teacher Education, 18*, 421-433.

Seitamo, L. (1991). *Psychological development in Arctic cultures*. Oulu: University of Oulu.

Sieber, J. (1993). The ethics and politics of sensitive research. In C. Renzetti & R. M. Lee (Eds.), *Researching sensitive topics* (pp. 14-26). London: Sage.

Sindell, P. S. (1997). Some discontinuities in the enculturation of Mistassini Cree children. In G. D. Spindler (Ed.), *Education and cultural process. Anthropological approaches* (pp. 383-392). Prospect Heights, IL: Waveland Press.

Skeggs, B. (1999a). Seeing differently: ethnography and explanatory power. *Australian Educational Research, 26*(1), 33-53.

Skeggs, B. (1999b). *Formations of class & gender*. London: SAGE.

Skutnabb-Kangas, T. (2009). *Literacy and oracy in mother-tongue based multi-lingual education.* Public lecture held in Mauritius, 24 October 2009.

Skutnabb-Kangas, T., & Dunbar, R. (2010). *Indigenous children's education as linguistic genocide and a crime against humanity? A global view.* Kautokeino: Resource Center for the Rights of Indigenous Peoples.

Smith, C. (Ed.) (2006). *Pohjoismainen saamelaissopimus: 13. marraskuuta 2002 nimitetyn suomalais-norjalais-ruotsalais- saamelaisen asiantuntijatyöryhmän 27. Lokakuuta 2005 luovuttama luonnos* [Nordic Sámi convention]. Oslo: Arbeids og inkluderingsdepartementet.

Smith, G. H. (2003). *Kaupapa Maori Theory: Theorizing indigenous transformation of education & schooling.* The University of Auckland & Te Whare Wananga o Awanuiarangi: Tribal-university; New Zealand. 'Kaupapa Maori Symposium' NZARE / AARE Joint Conference. Retrieved from http://www.aare.edu.au/03pap/pih03342.pdf

Smith, L. T. (2005). Building a research agenda for indigenous epistemologies and education. *Anthropology & Education Quarterly, 36*(1), 93–95.

Smith, L. T. (2012). *Decolonizing methodologies: research and indigenous peoples.* (2nd ed.) London: Zed Books.

Somekh, B. (2006). *Action research: a methodology for change and development.* Berkshire: Open University Press.

Spindler, G. D. (1997). Why have minority groups in North America been disadvantaged by their schools? In G. D. Spindler (Ed.), *Education and cultural process. Anthropological approaches* (pp. 96-109). (3rd ed.) Prospect Heights, IL: Waveland Press.

Spindler, G., & Hammond, L. (2000). The use of anthropological methods in education research: two perspectives. *Harvard Education Review, 70*(1), 39-48.

Spindler, G., & Spindler, L. (1997a). Ethnography. An anthropological view. In G. D. Spindler (Ed.), Education and cultural process. *Anthropological approaches* (pp. 50-55). Prospect Heights, IL: Waveland Press.

Spindler, G., & Spindler, L. (1997b). Cultural process and ethnography. An anthropological perspective. In G. D. Spindler (Ed.), *Education and cultural process. Anthropological approaches* (pp. 56-76). Prospect Heights, IL: Waveland Press.

Spivak, G. C. (1993). *Outside in the teaching machine.* New York, NY: Routledge.

Stiegelbauer, S. M. (1996). What is an elder? What do elders do? First nation elders as teachers in culture-based urban organization. *The Canadian Journal of Native Studies, 1*, 37–66.

Suoranta, J. (1999). Kasvatusantropologia ja (seikkailu)kasvatuksen tutkimus [Educational anthropology and research of (adventure)education]. In J. Suoranta (Ed.), *Nuorisotyöstä seikkailukasvatukseen [From juvenile work to adventure education]* (pp. 130-170). Tampere: Taju.

Tauli-Corpuz, V. (2009). The importance of Indigenous peoples in biodiversity conservation. Environment Matters 2009. *The World Bank Group. Annual review*, July 2008–June 2009 (fy09): 6-7.

Teasdale, G. R. (1995). Education and Culture: An Introduction. *Quarterly Review of Comparative Education, 96*(4), 587-592.

Todal, J. (2002). *"Jos fal gáhttet gollegielat": vitalisering av samisk språk i Noreg på 1990-talet ["If you saved your golden language": the revitalisation of Sámi language in Norway in the 1990s]*. Tromsø: Universitetet i Tromsø.

Tomal, D. R. (2003). *Action research for educators*. Lanham: Scarecrow Education.

Turner Strong, P. (2005). Recent ethnographic research on North American indigenous peoples. *The Annual Review of Anthropology, 34*, 253–268.

Turunen, T. (2008). *Mistä on esiopetussuunnitelmat tehty? Esiopetuksen opetus-suunnitelman perusteiden 1996 ja 2000 diskurssianalyyttinen tutkimus [From what is the curriculum for first grades made of? Discourse research about curriculum for first grades from 1996 and 2000]*. Rovaniemi: University of Lapland.

United Nations Declaration on Indigenous Peoples. (2007). United Nations. Retrieved from http://www.un.org/esa/socdev/unpfii/en/drip.html

United Nations Permanent Forum on Indigenous Issues. (2008). Indigenous Languages. United Nations. Retrieved from http://www.un.org/esa/socdev/unpfii/documents/Factsheet_languages_FINAL.pdf

Uusiautti, S., & Määttä, K. (2012). Can teachers teach children how to be moral? *British Journal of Education, Society & Behavioural Science, 2*(3), 260-270.

Uusikylä, K. (1980). *Miten kuvaan opetustapahtumaa [How do I describe the teaching event]*. Helsinki: Gaudeamus.

Valdiviezo, L. (2009). Bilingual intercultural education in indigenous schools: an ethnography of teacher interpretations of government policy. *International Journal of Bilingual Education and Bilingualism, 12*(1), 61-79.

Valkeapää, H. (1986). *Áppes 1 [ABC-book]*. Helsset: Skuvlaráddehus.

Valkonen, P., & Vilska, P. (2002). *Esikoululainen kielen käyttäjänä ja tutkijana [Preschooler as a language user and researcher]*. Joensuu: University of Joensuu.

Vilkuna, J. (2005). Kuka olet maailman ensimmäinen saamenkulttuurin professori? [Who are you, the world's first professor of Sámi culture?]. *Kaltio, 5*, 258.

Vygotsky, L. S. (1976). Play and its role in the mental development of the child. In J. S. Bruner, A. Jolly & K. Sylva (Eds.), *Play – its role in development and evolution* (pp. 537–554). New York, NY: Penguin Books.

Wardell, M. (2006) *Woolaning: an experiment in indigenous education*. Sydney: Macquarie University.

Webster, J. P., & John, T. A. (2010). Preserving a space for cross-cultural collaborations: an account of insider/outsider issues. *Ethnography and Education, 5*(2), 175-191.

Westman, A., & Utsi, J. E. (1998). *Gáriid áigi. Sámiid dološ gáriid ja oskku birra. Trumtid. Om samernas trummor och religion [Time of drum. About Sámi drums and spirit]*. Jokkmokk: Ájtte, Nordiska Museet.

Wimmer, R., Legare, L., Arcand, Y. & Cottrell, M. (2009). Experiences of beginning aboriginal teachers in band-controlled schools. *Canadian Journal of Education, 32*(4), 818-849.

Wolcott, H. F. (1997). The teacher as an enemy. In G. D. Spindler (Ed.), *Education and cultural process. Anthropological approaches* (pp. 77-92). (3rd ed.) Prospect Heights, IL: Waveland Press.

Wulf, C. (2002). *Anthropology of education: history and theory of anthropology*. Münster: Lit Verlag.

Wulf, C. (2008). Producing the social in rituals. Education and learning, mimesis and performativity. In P. Siljander, & A. Kivelä (Eds.), *Kasvatustieteen tila ja tutkimuskäytännöt: paradigmat katosivat, mitä jäljellä? [Status of education and research practices: paradigms disappeared, what is left?]* (pp. 51-71). Helsinki: Finnish Educational Research Association.

Yosso, T. J. (2006). *Critical race counterstories along the Chicana/Chicano educational pipeline*. New York, NY: Routledge.

Youdell, D. (2011). *School trouble, identity, power and politics in education*. London: Routledge.

Young, L., & Barrett, H. (2001). Adapting visual methods: action research with Kampala street children. *Area, 33*(2), 141-152.

Zahorik, J. A. (1975). The effect of planning on teaching. *The Elementary School Journal, 71*, 143–151.

Øzerk, K. (1999). *Opplæringsteori og læreplanforståelse: en opplæringsteoretisk, læreplanteoretisk og pedagogisk-filosofisk tilnærming til grunnskolens opplæringspraksis og de nye læreplanverkene L97 og L97 Samisk [Educational theory and curriculum understanding: an educational theory, curriculum theory and educational-philosophical approach to primary school teaching practice and the new curriculum works of L97 and L97 Sami]*. Vallset: Oplandske Bokforlag.

Øzerk, K. (2006). *Opplæringsteori og læreplanforståelse: en lærebok med vekt på kunnskapsløftet, rammeplan for barnehager og aktuelle kunnskaper for pedagoger [Educational theory and curriculum understanding: a textbook with an emphasis on knowledge promotion, curriculum for kindergarten and relevant knowledge for educators]*. Vallset: Oplandske Bokforlag.

Øzerk, K. (2010). *Samisk som mål og middel [Sámi as goal and tool]*. Paper presented at Sámi earenoámašpedagogalaš fágabeaivvit [Sámi special educational conference] 3 – 4 Mar 2010.

Authors

Pigga Keskitalo, Ph.D., works as the associate professor at the teacher training section of the Sámi University College (Sámi allaskuvla) in Kautokeino, Norway. Sámi University College has a special national responsibility over Sámi teacher training studies. Along with participating in the developmental projects of teaching, Keskitalo became interested in cultural sensitive teaching arrangements, and did her doctoral research about Sámi primary school issues, 'Cultural sensitivity in the Sámi School through educational anthropology' at the Faculty of Education, University of Lapland, Finland. Her research was funded by Sámi University College. Pigga Keskitalo is a Sámi teacher and researcher herself and lives in Enontekiö, northern Finland. She has published articles and books about Sámi education in many languages. (Photo by CJ Utsi)

Kaarina Määttä, Ph.D., is the professor of educational psychology at the Faculty of Education, University of Lapland, and deputy vice-chancellor at the University of Lapland, Finland. She supervised Pigga Keskitalo's and Satu Uusiautti's doctoral thesis and has written several international, peer-reviewed articles together with Pigga Keskitalo and Satu Uusiautti. She also is the supervisor of several forthcoming doctoral theses that analyze Sámi education. During her career, she has supervised over 50 doctoral theses, written hundreds of articles and dozens of text books, especially about love, human strengths, early childhood education and student guidance.

Satu Uusiautti, Ph.D., works as a specialist at University of Lapland, Finland, and as a post doctoral researcher in the research project *Love-based Leadership – An Interdisciplinary Approach* (http://www.ulapland.fi/lbleadership). Her personal research interests are in positive psychology and human strengths, happiness, success, and well-being in life in general but especially in the school world and diverse educational contexts.

www.ingramcontent.com/pod-product-compliance
Ingram Content Group UK Ltd.
Pitfield, Milton Keynes, MK11 3LW, UK
UKHW041140160426
5217IPUK00045B/28